FAITH AND CRISIS
IN THE STAGES OF LIFE

Adult Development and Christian Growth

James F. Cobble, Jr.

Faith and Crisis
in the Stages of Life

by James F. Cobble, Jr.

Hendrickson Publishers, Inc.
Peabody, Massachusetts

57111

Copyright © 1985
Hendrickson Publishers, Inc.
P.O. Box 3473, Peabody, MA 01961–3473
All rights reserved
Printed in the United States of America
ISBN 0-913 573-17-5

To my daughters
Emily Beth and Jessica Lynn,
who have taught me the true meaning of joy

Table of Contents

1
The Pilgrimage of Faith

One Saturday afternooon, while working in my backyard, I overheard the following conversation between my next door neighbor and his four-year-old son. The boy was playing in the driveway while his dad painted the garage.

"Daddy, can I go down to the park? Jimmy's at the park."

"No, I don't think so right now. I want you to stay here with dad."

"Why not? I wanna go down there. Jimmy gets to go."

"Jimmy's older than you are. I want you to stay here with me. Maybe we'll go down later."

"Dad, I wanna go now. If you loved me you'd let me go."

"Mickey, you know I love you. That's why I want you to stay here with me. Come over here and help dad paint the garage."

As I squatted to work in my rose garden, that conversation started me thinking about the love between a father and his son. I knew my neighbor loved his little boy very much. The boy also loved his father. I thought to myself, Can the love between Mickey and his dad really grow any deeper? When Mickey becomes an adult, will he be able to love his father any more than he does now as a four-year-old?

I knew that as Mickey aged his world would become more complicated.

He would experience more stress in his own life as well as in other important relationships. How could his love for his dad become any deeper or stronger than it was when he was a child?

Soon theological questions began to surface in my mind. One question seemed to trigger another. Do I love God more than I did when I first became a Christian twenty years ago? How is my love for him different today? How has my faith changed? How is it supposed to change? Am I supposed to have more faith today? Other questions followed.

I shared this story and these questions with a mature Christian friend in his early sixties.

"Ben," I asked, "Can a boy really love his father any more later in his life than he does now as a child? And what does that mean for our faith and love for God. Can it ever be stronger than it is when we first believe?"

After a brief silence, Ben looked at me and spoke.

"Jim, if that boy at age twenty loved his father like he did when he was four years old, it would be an immature relationship. Our love grows by changing to meet the new needs of life. The needs of a twenty-year-old are different than a four-year-old's. His love must mature as he matures as a boy and as a man."

Ben continued, "The same is true with our relationship with God. Faith and love must mature. That means they must change to meet the needs of life."

That conversation started me to think more about the relationship between faith and aging. As we age, how does faith in God adapt to the changing circumstances of life? How does faith develop? Does it increase as we mature, and if so, what does that mean in practice? Or is faith something that is renegotiated throughout life as we face new and changing realities? Do faith issues, which we believe to have been settled once and for all, reappear in new forms later in life to challenge and provoke us? Is the nature of our faith related to our age? What about people who become Christians later in life—does their faith develop differently than those who become Christians at a younger age? Do people of the same age face similar faith issues, regardless of how long they have been Christians? And finally, what difference does Christian faith make in responding to the changing realities of life? If life affects the development of our faith, how does faith affect the development of our lives? What kind of changes can we expect throughout adulthood?

Until recently, it was assumed that adulthood was a period of relative stability. Now it is recognized that we all experience important transitions throughout life. These life changes have become the focus of much attention.

For the most part, life has traditionally been divided into four periods. The first was the preschool years. The chief tasks of this period were to explore the world through the body and the senses and to develop beginning language skills. We thought of this as a time for playing games and watching Captain Kangaroo. If you were really bright you could count to ten and say your ABC's by the time you were four.

Next came going to school. The development of social skills and the acquisition of knowledge were critical to this phase. During the next twelve to sixteen years we were supposed to learn everything we would ever need to know. Of course there were a few tidbits of knowledge we would pick up here and there later in life, but basically we were done with school. In essence, that meant that our education was finished.

Then came finding a job, getting married, and settling down. That meant establishing our career, becoming parents and rearing a family. This was to take up about the next forty-five years. Television programs like *Father Knows Best, Leave It to Beaver,* and *My Three Sons* showed us how it was to be done.

The last stage was retirement. This was a time when we would leave our jobs and then disappear. No one really knew what was to happen during this period of life. We might receive a gold watch so we would know what time it was. Apparently, people were perceived to have nothing but ''time on their hands.''

Was life really that simple? No way! It may have been less complicated in certain respects, but human beings have always experienced many transitions throughout the life cycle. Today it is recognized that we continue to change and develop throughout life. Some changes are easy to cope with. Others are not. What we discover is that life is a mixture of change and stability. When things are stable we feel more secure and in control. When major changes occur, we feel more stress and tension.

No two human beings experience life in exactly the same way. Yet certain aspects of development are shared by most people. As we explore the relationship between adult development and Christian growth, we will discover the richness, diversity and common dimensions of our lives and of our faith in God. The story of Edith, which is found below, reflects many of the major changes which emerge during eighty-one years of living. As a Christian, Edith embraced her life as a gift from God.

The Pilgrimage of Faith

Edith, Age Eighty-one

"We'll, I'm eighty-one years old and I'd say I'm a happy person. I do get lonesome sometimes. Don't you get tired of sad stories? I'm not like that. I pray, 'Lord, let me show forth your sunlight and joy!' I'm glad the Lord has given me that nature. I give my trials to God and not to someone else.

"Anyway, I was born in 1901. We were all raised in a Christian home and I always felt a hunger for the Lord. When I was eight years old I became a member of the Methodist church. We had some good meetings back in those days.

"When I was eighteen-and-a-half I married Henry. He was quite a bit older than me and was a farmer. A year later Lisel was born; altogether we had six children.

"When we got married we were only taking in about fifteen dollars a week. We had some land but Henry decided he wanted to sell it and move down to Kentucky. That was about 1927.

"We went ahead and auctioned off the farm and just about everything we owned. We headed on down to Kentucky but things just didn't turn out like we hoped. We weren't there too long and decided to come back to Illinois. When we got back Henry took all of our money down to the bank. There were a lot of people there trying to get their money out, but Henry didn't know what was going on. He just put our money in the bank and we ended up losing every penny of it. That was right when the Great Depression hit. We didn't have much, but the Lord provided for every need.

"After that we moved several times and ended up in California. During this whole time we were always in church. We even had prayer meetings in our home. When you raise your children in the atmosphere of prayer and praise, they won't get away from the Lord!

"Lisel, our oldest daughter, got married in '41. Things were going okay for us, but we decided to move back to Illinois in '48. All six children were on their own by now and it was just me and Henry.

"The next thing that really stands out in my mind is our oldest son committed suicide in 1954. He got sick and just lost his mind. The whole family was torn up. Everybody blamed themself. Sometimes there comes a time in life when nobody can help.

"We moved back to California after the suicide. I guess it was just hard to be in Illinois after that. We bought up a chicken farm, but we only stayed there three years. The freeway came through and forced us out. We moved back to Illinois again in '58. We moved again two years later.

"Henry died in 1972. We thought he had a cold, but it turned out to be cancer. The doctor told me but we didn't tell Henry right off. I told the kids, though.

"Our youngest daughter was visiting with us at the time. We knew we were going to have to tell him and Mildred wanted to be the one to do it. I had to work that morning so I said, 'Go ahead and tell daddy while I'm out.'

"When I got back at lunch time he was sitting in the living room on the sofa. I sat down next to him and said, 'Did Mid tell you what the doctor said?'

"He said, 'Yes, but can't they take it out or do something?'

"I said, 'No, it's just spread too far.'

"He never said another word.

"Christmas dinner was the last meal he ate at the table. We set up a bed for him in the living room and I would stay up night and day with him. We finally had to take him to the hospital. That was the hardest thing I ever did. I knew that when we took him out of the house, that he'd never be coming back.

"I was with him when he died. I was standing there at the end of his bed. I looked over at the nurse and said, 'He's now walking on the streets of glory.' The nurse began to cry.

"All through our lives we walked with the Lord. I'm here today because of the Lord Jesus. Maybe I shouldn't say this, but when you have a big family you're always planning for them and their future. There is more to look forward to. Now it gets lonesome. We had six children in ten years. We were busy all the time. Now when you're not busy it makes a difference. It's important to keep busy, but it should be worthwhile. I can't stand those TV shows. I want real things in my life.

"What keeps me going now is the presence of the Lord and the church. When you're alone you don't have someone to talk things over with before you go to bed or when you wake up. I talk to God. The Lord is just there. Many nights I'll quote the whole Ninety-first Psalm before I go to sleep. I don't know what people do who don't know the Lord. What kind of future do they have to look forward to?

"The only thing I try to do now is to be more of a blessing to someone else. We shouldn't just think of our own needs, but we need to think about others. I've been making quilt blocks for the girls.''

Summary

Edith and Henry experienced many transitions during their adult years. They passed through family and financial crises. Several times they pulled up roots to become established elsewhere. Together they faced Henry's illness knowing that he would die. Now Edith, in her eighties, manages on a modest income and spends more time alone. She's not as busy as she used to be. Throughout her life, Edith's faith proved to be a stablizing and sustaining force. At age eighty-one, she still looks forward to the future.

Like Edith and Henry, you and I are going to face transitions and changes throughout life. Some will be stressful. Others may produce a crisis or bring joy. Generally, though, they will come whether we are ready for them or not.

Many, but not all transitions in life are predictable. It is possible to equip ourselves to successfully face challenges throughout the life cycle. One purpose of this book is to help you understand some of the main developmental issues and tasks associated with each stage of the adult life cycle. Such knowledge can be useful in understanding and anticipating your own development as well as the development of others around you.

The major theme running throughout this book, though, is that faith can and should make a difference in how we respond to life events. But it is also true that life events affect the development of faith. There is a mutual interaction that takes place. Throughout the course of this book we will examine the lives and faith of Christians as they encounter issues related to leaving home, selecting a career, getting married, rearing children, changing careers, facing health problems, dealing with divorce, losing loved ones—in essence, the issues of life. We shall pay special attention to the question, How does faith change with age?

We shall begin by examining the stages of life.

2
The Stages of Life

I will never forget the birth of our daughter. Jan woke me at 5:27 A.M. Excitedly she announced, "Jim, my water just broke!" Immediately I leaped out of bed. I thought to myself, Get the book! Get the book! Find out what you're supposed to do!

There it was—the Lamaze book with all the answers. Somehow we made it. Twelve hours later Jan gave birth to a beautiful six-pound three-ounce baby girl. In those first moments together, as we held our newborn daughter, I experienced the joy, delicacy, and mystery of life. It was all lying there right in front of me, embodied in a tiny little person—flesh of my flesh and bone of my bone. As I gazed upon those miniature ears, fingernails, and toes—all so perfectly formed—I was aware of the miracle of life. The life cycle was being renewed.

The human life cycle progresses in just one direction, from birth to death. The life cycle itself is made up of various stages or eras. The earliest stages include infancy, childhood, and adolescence. The later stages can be divided into early, middle, and later adulthood.

There are many aspects to our development as we pass from one stage to another. We may also experience a host of changes within any particular stage. Since these changes affect both the development and expression of faith, a clear understanding of human development can aid us in our own understanding of Christian growth. There is no single theory that satisfactorily explains or encompasses the totality of adult development. However, several viewpoints do exist that provide us with a starting point for this task. Three of these theories will be discussed below.

The discussion that follows is not intended to be used as a blueprint to see if specific individuals are on-course as they move through the life cycle. Hopefully though, it will help all of us to reflect on our own development and it will better equip us to deal with the past, present and future. In addition, while the Bible provides us with the necessary guidance and instruction concerning spiritual growth, an understanding of adult development will aid us in reflecting about our growth as Christians. Such an understanding has implications for counseling, preaching, teaching, evangelism, worship, fellowship—the totality of the Church's life and mission. First, though, let us examine the stages of life.

Erik Erickson: Eight Stages of Life

Erik Erickson spent his early adulthood in Vienna where he was trained as a teacher and later as a child psychoanalyst. After Hitler came to power, Erickson emigrated to the United States where he established a worldwide reputation in the field of developmental psychology.

Erickson maintained that as we move through the life cycle, from birth to death, we pass through eight major periods of life.[1] Each stage is characterized by a struggle between two opposing tendencies. For example, in the first period, *Infancy*, the two opposing tendencies are trust and mistrust. Erickson believed that if a child is to experience a healthy psychological development later in life, then he or she must learn to trust as an infant. This was to be accomplished primarily through maternal care. As the child's needs were met, trust would be nurtured and promoted. The child would then be better prepared to cope with the developmental tasks of the next period of life.

Each of the eight stages of life is characterized by a crisis or turning point. By ''crisis'' Erickson meant a critical point of decision which leads either to personal growth or decline. If growth occurs, e.g., if the positive tendency trust wins out over the negative tendency mistrust, then the individual is able to focus his or her energies on the next stage of development. However, if the negative tendency wins out, then the next stage of development becomes all the more difficult. In fact, psychological problems may surface.

The eight stages are not neatly differentiated in actual experience and Erickson believed that a person generally was not located in any single stage at a given time. Most people tend to vascillate between at least two stages. This oscillation is conditioned by both social and psychological factors, and the ensuing struggles are both conscious and unconscious in nature. Erickson classified his eight stages in the following categories:

1. *Infancy*

The struggle is between trust and mistrust. Maternal care should help nuture trust. This stage continues until about age two.

2. *Early Childhood*

The two opposing tendencies are *autonomy* on the one hand and *shame and doubt* on the other. During this stage the child begins to exert its own will. The challenge is to help it develop a sense of self-control without a loss of self-esteem.

3. *Play Age*

The struggle revolves around *initiative* and *guilt*. During this period, the child, guided by its conscience, is to develop a sense of initiative, vision and enterprise. He or she is to be able to pursue childhood goals without being paralyzed by feelings of guilt or fear of punishment.

4. *School Age*

This stage is characterized by *industry* versus *inferiority*. In order to successfully enter the adult world, a child must learn how to be a worker and a potential provider. However, if the child develops feelings of inadequacy or discouragement, it will affect the ability to learn and work.

5. *Adolescence*

The two opposing tendencies are *identity* and *identity confusion*. As a sense of identity emerges, the adolescent is able to move into the adult world as a responsible and productive member of society. The negative side is confusion concerning one's identity in various life roles.

6. *Young Adulthood*

The crisis involves *intimacy* versus *isolation*. The young adult discovers the need for love, not only sexual, but also love nurtured in faithful partnerships that may call for significant sacrifices and commitments. Such intimacy is unlikely without a clear sense of identity (stage 5). The alternative to intimacy is isolation.

7. *Maturity*

The seventh stage of life, which may be the longest, involves a struggle between *generativity* and *stagnation*. By generativity, Erickson meant establishing and guiding the next generation. It includes not only becoming a parent, but of making one's mark in the world. It also entails showing care and concern for the next generation. Without a sense of generativity, stagnation and boredom may set in.

8. *Old Age*

The final stage is characterized by *integrity* versus *despair*. Integrity is identified with emotional integration and an affirmation of one's life and meaning. Despair arises out of feelings of "meaninglessness" and from a sense that time is too short to do anything about it.

Erickson devoted most of his attention to the first twenty years of life. Most researchers would now agree that the adult years are more complex in their design and development and see a greater number of developmental periods in adulthood than did Erickson. Two such theories will be examined below.

Else Frenkel–Brunswick

The Five Stages of the Life Cycle

Else Frenkel–Brunswick divided the life cycle into five stages.[2] Four of these stages are oriented toward adulthood.

Stage One. During this period the child lives at home. Life revolves around a narrow group of interests including school and family.

Stage Two. The second period begins between the sixteenth and twentieth years of life. The key turning point occurs when the individual leaves home and engages in independent activity. This includes the development of new personal relationships. This period, which usually lasts until age twenty-eight, is simply preparatory for the third stage.

Stage Three. This stage begins somewhere between the twenty-sixth and thirtieth years of life; it is usually the longest and involves critical choices and commitments. Definite decisions must be made concerning vocation and the establishment of a home and family. This period is the most fruitful with respect to professional and creative work. It also represents the highest point of social interaction. Stage three ends at approximately fifty years of age.

Stage Four. This period, which begins at about forty-eight, is associated with a greater number of negative dimensions. Psychological crises, sickness, and the death of friends and associates are experienced during this stage with greater frequency than before.

Stage Five. Frequently introduced by retirement, the fifth stage commences at about age sixty-four. Hobbies, retrospections, focus on death, and philosophical reflection mark this period.

Frenkel-Brunswick tended to focus more upon the developmental issues revolving around family, career and so on. Erickson dealt more with the psychosocial issues. Our final theory discussed below attempts to integrate both of these dimensions of human development.

Daniel Levinson: The Seasons of Life

Daniel Levinson and his associates have developed one of the most comprehensive theories of the adult life cycle.[3] Although Levinson's study focused exclusively on males, it does have important theoretical considerations relevant to females. Also, the study did not extend beyond the decade of the forties. Nevertheless, it perhaps provides, the best starting point currently available for understanding the nature of change in the adult years. Levinson's theoretical framework will help us later as we examine the nature of faith development.

Daniel Levinson divides the life cycle into the following four eras:
1. Childhood and Adolescence: age 0–22
2. Early Adulthood: age 17–45
3. Middle Adulthood: age 40–65
4. Late Adulthood: age 60–?

Each era of life is similar to the acts of a play or to the major divisions within a novel.[4] The four eras provide the "big picture." However, in order to understand more completely the nature of adult development, it is necessary to zero in on the particular developmental periods that occur within each era of life. Generally, each of the above eras can be subdivided into four developmental periods. Levinson's research focused on the two eras of early and middle adulthood.

Early Adulthood: Ages 17-45

Early adulthood is the second era of the life cycle. During this span of life major choices are made concerning family and career. Biological functioning reaches its peak sometime during the twenties and then begins a gradual decline. By age forty, individuals become more aware of health concerns.

Early adulthood is full of critical events, such as leaving home, entering a career, selecting a mate, becoming a parent, establishing a household, rearing children, settling down, and climbing the ladder toward personal achievement and success. Critical choices concerning one's life and future must often be made at a time when one is least prepared to make them. The timing of significant events like marriage may be pressured by social expectations. Levinson identifies four distinct periods in the era of early adulthood.

Early adult transition, ages 17-22. This period has two primary tasks: (1) leaving the pre-adult world and (2) initiating early adulthood. The first task involves separating from one's family as well as modifying or terminating relationships with other important persons or groups. This may unfold in many different ways, such as leaving home to go to college, joining the army, or moving to start a new job. The redefinition of relationships may often result in a sense of personal loss. It may lead to anger, depression, or a new sense of freedom.

The second task of initiating early adulthood is necessary in order to establish a basis for living in the adult world. This may include further training, such as enrolling in college or becoming an apprentice in a particular trade. The young adult must examine the world and begin to define his or her options concerning important life decisions. As the young adult enters the next developmental phase, firmer choices and commitments will begin to be made. In turn, this will lead to a greater sense of self-definition and direction in life.

Entering the adult world, ages 22-28. The key challenge during this period is to fashion and to test an initial structure for one's life. This means moving from being a son or daughter to becoming a novice, self-supporting adult. Levinson identifies two major tasks for this period: (1) exploring alternative options and (2) creating a stable life structure.

The novice adult is confronted by a world which provides multiple options. Often captivated by a new sense of freedom and adventure, the young adult begins to test the available options before making firm commitments. This sense of exploration may affect career decisions, sexual relationships, financial obligations, and travel plans as well as personal values and commitments.

Yet at the same time, there are mounting social pressures and expectations to make firm choices and commitments. This is especially true concerning marriage and career. The young adult may experience an internal need to develop a more organized life and to begin to define and to initiate life goals.

The two tasks of exploring options and creating stability often contribute to a feeling of personal tension. Some individuals may go to one extreme by leading a totally transient life while others may make early and strong commitments concerning marriage and career. Most individuals probably fall somewhere between these two extremes. Toward the end of this period, many individuals will begin to rethink initial choices as they move into the age thirty transition. There is a growing sense that important decisions remain to be made. This may be accompanied by feelings that parts of the self have been neglected. Levinson notes that many experience a moderate crisis during the first two developmental periods of early adulthood. This is not surprising in light of the number of major decisions that are made during these two periods of development.

The age 30 transition, ages 28–33. This period serves as a bridge between entering the adult world and settling down as an adult. It is a time for reflection on and evaluation of initial choices and commitments. If necessary, it is a time to begin modification of one's life structure. Three important questions surface during this period:[5]

1. What have I done with my life?
2. What do I want to make of it?
3. What new directions shall I choose?

If one's earlier choices have proven to be satisfactory and on target with goals and values, the transition may proceed smoothly without any major disruptions. However, if there is a sense of significant despair about the pattern of one's life, it may give rise to a serious redefinition of goals, commitments, and values. This may lead to traumatic changes in both career and family life. Such a transition may prove to be both painful and costly.

The settling down period, ages 33–40. This stage brings the era of early adulthood to a close. Like the other periods before it, this one is also characterized by two developmental tasks: (1) to establish one's niche in society and (2) to work at advancement.

The object of the first task is to develop stability in one's life, family, and career. It is a time to put down roots and to become an established member of one's community and profession. The objective of the second task is to work at advancement, i.e. to climb the ladder of success. Levinson notes that the goal can be a number of possibilities including wealth, power, prestige, recognition, achievement, or the establishment of particular forms of family life and community involvement.

Levinson divides the settling down period into two distinct phases: (1) Early Settling Down, and (2) Late Settling Down. Early Settling Down is characterized by becoming a junior member of society. The goal is to get on with the work; to climb the ladder of success; to get married if one is still single. After three or four years the second phase begins. This phase is characterized by "becoming one's own man." The goal is to become a senior member of society; to be more independent; to have more authority; to speak with one's own voice. As the culmination of early adulthood, the Settling Down Period is critical for launching the individual into mid-life.

Middle Adulthood, Ages 40–60

There is no one event that signals the arrival of middle adulthood. Rather, the cumulative force of several factors indicate that one is middle-aged. While bodily decline is gradual, and almost imperceptible during the late twenties and thirties, key changes often occur during the forties, which bring about a heightened awareness that one is aging. In addition to aches and pains, it is common to experience a decline in vision and hearing. The graying of hair, the losing of teeth, or the wrinkling of skin can intensify the feelings of becoming older.

There is also what Levinson describes as the "sequence of generations." The middle-aged individual is a bridge between two generations. A person in his or her forties is viewed by the younger generation as part of the "establishment." He or she now takes on the parent-image rather than that of a "buddy." The sight of aging parents and dying friends or associates may intensify feelings of mortality.

During this phase of life, the home becomes a launching pad for sending children into the adult world. Family roles tend to change as children leave the soon-to-be empty nest. Women formerly outside of the labor force may return to work. Menopause normally occurs around age forty-seven.

At around age forty, a man will often make a serious evaluation of his own career. Levinson identifies three prominent questions that surface during this time:[6]

1. What have I done?
2. Where am I now?
3. Of what value is my life to society, to other persons, and especially to myself?

If a man has achieved his goals he must ask, what now? If he has not reached them, he must assess how realistic his goals actually are. On one hand, this may result in a major, all-out effort to obtain them, that is characterized by a "now or never" attitude. On the other hand, feelings of failure, despair, or defeat may be so overwhelming that a gradual surrender to one's position in life results.

Just as he did in the early adulthood period, Levinson identified four distinct periods within middle adulthood. However, his study only focused on the first two—the mid-life transition and the entrance into middle adulthood.

Mid-life transition, ages 40–45. This period has three main tasks: (1) to terminate the era of early adulthood; (2) to initiate middle adulthood; and (3) to deal with conflicting feelings and values brought about by middle age.

During the mid-life transition, a person fluctuates between two different eras. Feelings of youth and immortality begin to give way to an awareness of aging and mortality. One major task of the mid-life transition is to reappraise personal goals and dreams in light of a new understanding of the future. This involves a process which Levinson calls *de-illusionment.*[7] Levinson maintains that illusions play a vital role in shaping our lives. Illusions are assumptions and beliefs about one's self and the world which are not true. During the era of early adulthood, illusions may play a significant role in shaping personal goals and commitments. For example, many college athletes live under the illusion that someday they will become professional athletes. Young writers may dream of winning the Pulitzer Prize. Others may cultivate illusions related to political power, business achievement, or financial independence. During the mid-life transition, illusions concerning career, finances, family life, and other important aspects of one's dream may begin to yield to the realities of one's circumstances and options. While this may result in feelings of pain or loss, it can also stir up sensations of relief and freedom. Whereas early adulthood stimulates the formation and development of illusions, middle adulthood tends to bring a person more face to face with the feasibility of personal goals and aspirations.

The second major task is to develop a new pattern of life which will provide stability and meaning for middle age. This entails modification of goals, commitments, relationships, and perceptions in order to support the emerging tasks of middle adulthood. Changes in family life, caring for and facing the death of loved ones, career concerns, and an increased awareness of aging and bodily decline contribute to both outward adaptation and inward reflection.

According to Levinson, the final developmental task of this transition period is to resolve conflicting feelings concerning fundamental polarities. One polarity is the tension between young/old. Individuals in the mid-life transition still want to think of themselves as "young," but other social indicators begin to identify them as "old." For that reason, Jack Benny always claimed to be thirty-nine.

Another polarity is the tension between destruction/creation. On the one hand, feelings of death and mortality begin to surface. Yet on the other hand, there is the drive to make a lasting contribution to one's family, profession, society, and the generation to come. Other polarities may also emerge which contribute to feelings of tension or conflict.

Entering middle adulthood, ages 45–50. The main developmental task of this period is to bring stability and meaning to one's commitments and values as a middle-aged person. If the mid-life transition has proceeded according to expectations and without any great upheavals, this period will be a time to build upon commitments and choices that have already been established. However, if the transition was marked by crisis and trauma, it may be a time for rebuilding and reestablishing a meaningful structure to one's life. Levinson's study concludes with this period.

Summary

Each of the above perspectives on human development provides us with important insights relevant to the study of Christian growth. No one claims to be making a statement that "this is the way it is" for everyone. Yet it is true that as unique human beings we also share much with other members of the human race.

Christians are not immune from the normal tasks associated with the various stages of life. Like all other human beings, we must deal with concerns related to family life, career, health, aging, the care of elderly parents, and unexpected tragedies as well as a multitude of other issues.

The fundamental question is, when actually facing these issues, what difference does it make to be a Christian? What role does faith play in the life development of Christians? Furthermore, how do the various developmental tasks that we encounter across the span of life affect the development and expression of faith? We shall begin an exploration of these questions as we examine the concept of life structure.

3
The Structure of Life

One evening a few of the teenagers in our neighborhood dropped by to visit my wife Jan and me. We were sitting and talking in the living room and had somehow gotten on the topic of comedians.

Jan said, "I've always liked Jack Benny. I wish his programs were still on TV."

"Who's Jack Benny. I've never heard of him," replied Michelle.

"Yeah," her friend said. "Me either."

At first I thought to myself, You've got to be kidding. Where've you been all your life? Then it hit me. They don't know who he is because they weren't even alive when he was on TV or radio. The fact is you're getting older and the world is changing.

The truth is, the world is changing faster than any of us realize. Prior to the fifteenth century, social change was slow. From the perspective of the individual, little change could be noticed within one's lifetime. The pace of life was unhurried. News traveled slowly. The main sources of transportation were ships, horses, and feet.

The next five hundred years witnessed dramatic changes in human lifestyles. The printing press was invented. Stock companies and large scale international trade developed. Galileo, Newton, and others revolutionized science. The industrial age prompted urban growth and the escalation of factories. Technology has totally altered modern life.

The entire household was refashioned in two decades (1912-1932) by the use of electrical appliances.[1] The automobile, radio, and television transformed human activity in the span of one generation. The computer can now be added to this list. Change is taking place more rapidly than ever before.

Knowledge doubles about every ten years. Those who work in professional or technical fields must regularly continue their education or face the risk of becoming obsolete. People must be prepared to become retrained for a new occupation because of the changing nature of both our knowledge and our economy.

Our world is different from that of our parents'; our children's world will be different from what we now know. Society has changed dramatically within our own lifetime. Think of the differences between the "roaring" of the twenties, the depression of the thirties, the world war of the forties, the American dream of the fifties, the civil strife of the sixties, and Watergate and the energy crises of the seventies. We can already sense the importance of concerns related to nuclear warfare and global economic issues taking shape for the eighties.

No one knows how our world will be different ten years from today, but it will change. And those changes, whether they are social, political, technical, military, environmental, or economic will alter not only how you and I live, the entire human race will be affected.

As we can see, the nature of our environment influences the structure of our lives. Most of us notice few changes in our lives from one day to the next. Yet, over time significant changes do occur. The concept of *life structure* helps us to understand the fundamental changes that arise in a person's life over time. Developed by Daniel Levinson, this concept focuses upon the underlying fabric of a person's life. A life structure is "the basic pattern or design of a person's life at any given time."[2] The primary task within any stage or era of life is to build or modify one's life structure. The rapidly changing nature of our environment makes this an ongoing task.

Every individual makes critical choices throughout life based upon an underlying set of values and perceptions about one's self and the world. Our lives become embedded in a resulting network of relationships and commitments. A person's marriage, family, hobbies, dreams, social roles, and so on become an expression of these choices and values. The overall design or pattern of these choices, values, commitments, and relationships make up one's life structure.

A related concept is that of *life space*.[3] Life space refers to the scope and complexity of our environment. It includes the actual geographical space in which we live out our lives as well as all of the relationships we maintain by personal contact, letter, or telephone.

Our life space is three-dimensional.[4] The dimensions include number, intensity, and complexity. Number refers to how many relationships we maintain at any given time. Intensity corresponds to how emotionally involved or committed we are to any given relationship. Complexity indicates how intricate our relationships are with respect to various groups or individuals. By identifying the patterns and dimensions of our life space, it is possible to develop a life map. This map represents the social reality in which we live.

Simply changing one aspect of life does not necessarily alter one's life structure although it may affect one's life space. Moving from one city to another brings about many changes and requires a person to adapt, but it does not necessarily alter the fundamental fabric of one's existence. For the life structure to change, basic modifications must occur in the way one embraces life.

In one sense, our life structure is like a tent. Although this is an oversimplified illustration, it will help to get the point across. The tent pegs represent our most important commitments, values, perceptions, and relationships. These may include our faith, family, job, health, friendships, and so one. If we are camping and one tent peg comes loose, we don't worry that the tent will collapse. However, if three or four pegs come out of the ground at the same time, we fear that the whole thing may come down.

Our life structure is similar to the tent illustration. If one of the "pegs" of our life becomes loose—for example, we may change jobs—we can handle it better if the other "pegs" remain firmly in place. But if we change jobs, have marital difficulties, and face major surgery all at once, we may feel like our tent is collapsing. During these times we must alter our life structure in order to deal adequately with both personal and environmental concerns. Often this occurs during transitional periods which may last four or five years.

Developmental Periods

Each stage or era of life can be subdivided into shorter developmental periods. Levinson, for example, divides early adulthood into four developmental periods. Each new era of life begins with a transition period and then is followed by a period of stability. According to Levinson, this alternating pattern continues throughout life. During the stable periods, which last six or seven years but rarely more than ten, the primary task is to build, to strengthen, or to modify one's life structure. Then transitional periods, which last four or five years, are times of soul-searching, questioning, reappraising, and exploring new options. The main task of transitional periods is to review commitments and choices made earlier in life and to consider what changes, if any, need to be made as one prepares for the next period of life.

Transitions

While we go through major developmental periods where our life structure is modified, we also experience transitions during stable periods as well. For example, transitions occur as we adjust social roles, like getting married or taking a new job. Such transitions arise whenever our life space is altered.

Some transitions in life are predictable, like leaving home, getting married, becoming a parent, experiencing menopause, and so on. Other transitions occur unexpectedly, like those caused by illness, injury, or death. Normally, unexpected transitions cause more stress and tension than do those for which we can plan.

Life transitions, then, occur in two fundamental ways. The first is an extended transitional period which may last four or five years. During that time, the basic patterns or designs of our lives change. These periods often begin several years before the ages 20, 30, 40, 50, and 60. They may arise at other ages as well. Each transitional period is followed by a time of greater stability reflecting firmer choices and commitments.

The second way transitions occur is through particular changes in life like marriage or retirement. These transitions do not necessarily alter one's life structure, although they may require adaptation. Some transitions are predictable while others happen unexpectedly. Such transitions often serve as "marker events" or "milestones."

Milestones

Milestones are important marker events that occur during one's lifetime. They may stand out in our memory as significant reference points. One such event for the nation of Israel was its being led out of Egypt. The prophets frequently refer to this (Jer. 2:6; Dan. 9:15; Amos 2:10). Another milestone was the crossing of the Jordan River. A pile of twelve stones was set up as a lasting reminder to future generations of what God had done for his people (Josh. 4:7). We each experience important milestones throughout life.

Many of us recall our childhood in relationship to what grade we were in at school. Each grade level stands out as a marker which we use to recall specific memories and events. As we enter the adult world, we tend to mark-off life according to particular events. These may include graduations, marriages, accidents, retirement, job changes, or moves.

As we grow older, time seems to pass by more quickly. In part, this may be explained by the fact that important reference points occur with less regularity and are less associated with age. A favorite phrase among adults is, "It seems like only yesterday," when it was actually years ago.

Developmental Tasks

Each stage of life, as well as each developmental period, has its own particular tasks and issues.[5] Infants must learn to crawl, walk, and eventually to speak. Children must develop social skills. Adolescents must begin to prepare for adult life and develop a sense of personal identity.

We continue to encounter new tasks and issues during the adult years. For example, there are many tasks associated with courtship, marriage, becoming parents, and rearing children. Later in life we must deal with the loss of loved ones as well as facing our own death. In short, developmental tasks are present throughout the entire life cycle.

To some extent, the successful achievement of current and future tasks is related to how well we have responded to tasks earlier in life. For example, a child's social development is related to the earlier task of learning to communicate. An adult will find the tasks of marriage and family life difficult if he or she has never developed a sense of personal identity. Failure in current or past tasks can contribute to frustration, disappointment, or difficulties in the future. However, depending upon one's outlook on life and willingness to change, opportunities for personal growth are always present. This fundamental truth is at the heart of the gospel.

Developmental tasks occur in a variety of ways. Some tasks are biological and take place early in life as our bodies mature and develop. Other biological tasks confront us later in life as we experience bodily deterioration. Still other tasks are social in nature. Social tasks occur throughout life as we relate to individuals, groups, and institutions. We also encounter psychological tasks related to our emotional development and self-awareness. These tasks are critical since they affect our self-perception and self-expression.

Not only do we develop socially, physically, and psychologically, we also develop spiritually. Christians are to press on toward maturity and perfection (Phil. 3:12-16; Matt. 5:48). Some developmental tasks related to our faith include engaging in good works, growing in our knowledge of Christ, becoming more self-controlled, learning to persevere, developing a godly character, expressing kindness, and manifesting love. Growth in these areas will lead to a productive and fruitful life (2 Pet. 1:5-11).

Our spiritual growth is similar to our physical growth and social development. If we fail in the achievement of certain tasks, we will discover other tasks to be all the more difficult. As one fellow put it, "You can't learn algebra until you know your ABC's." The writer of the book of Hebrews said it this way: ". . . though by this time you ought to be teachers, you need someone to teach you the elementary truths of God's word all over again. You need milk, not solid food!" (5:12).

From the many interviews that I have conducted, I am convinced that our growth as Christians is very much related to our development as adults. There is a tendency to look to God for help and guidance during periods of transition and uncertainty or when we face tasks beyond our scope to handle. These times can be stepping stones to personal growth and maturity. For some, though, as soon as the crisis is over God is forgotten. They develop a mentality of "foxhole" Christianity. This is illustrated in the story of Ron and Lisa found below. At first God was simply a source of help in a time of trouble. Later, their relationship with God took on a more profound meaning.

Ron and Lisa McDonald, ages 32 and 31

Lisa: "I was raised in church, but I really never knew what it was about. My mother took me and the only reason I joined was because my girl friend did. My relationship with God was shallow.

"Ron and I got married when I was nineteen and he was drafted eight months later. A week before he left to go to Vietnam we found out I was pregnant. That was a real crisis and I began to seek God.

"I started reading the Bible and praying for Ron because I was afraid. I was desperate. I began to seek God. I couldn't understand the King James Version so I bought a Living Bible. That was the closest relationship with God I ever had.

"When Ron finally came home, everything was a mess. He had nightmares and began to drink. He couldn't accept the fact that he had an eight-month-old baby. If it hadn't been for my experience in the Lord, we couldn't have made it. We felt like strangers.

"During that two-year period I had to hang on to God with everything I had. I wanted to give up many times, but God wouldn't let me.

"Later Ron became a Christian and I got more shallow. The crisis was behind us. In fact, I began to fight God. Ron began to go to church and I started getting frustrated. I would start fights on Sunday before church. I felt like I was losing control. Ron was getting higher on the spiritual ladder than me and I resented it. I even began being mean to our two-year-old daughter."

Ron: "I always believed that God was real, but I didn't know how to apply it. I didn't believe anybody could live for God.

"My wife and I were married at the Methodist church. Then I got drafted. The military challenged me beyond my endurance to stand. When I came back from Vietnam I had a real guilt trip. The reality of God still haunted me. I didn't want to be around Christians.

"This one guy started working with me and there was something different about him. He became a friend and later started to talk to me about God. I was trying to readjust from Vietnam and was also having marital problems.

"He invited me to church and when I went I gave my life to Christ. I really meant it. My wife was more of a Christian than I was and when I took her to church she began to fight it. She knew I was a rascal, but the people at church treated me like a brother.

"I saw how consecrated other people were and that challenged me. The more I would seek God, the closer he would draw to me. I prayed, 'Lord use me.' That was ten years ago. Since then I've gone to college and now I'm a minister."

Lisa: "Later, as Ron began to grow I saw my problem was pride. I began to put my faith back in the Lord. Our faith began to grow together. It didn't happen all at once, though.

"I became more mature. The first time I turned to God it was in desperation. Even though I prayed to God I had to control things. It was different this time. I realized that I had to rest in the Lord and do it his way. We were still being tested, but it was different. It wasn't learning if God was real, but I was finding answers.''

At first, Lisa's faith was affected by circumstances. In fact, she embraced faith because of them. Later, though, her circumstances were affected by her faith. She and Ron moved beyond circumstances to a stable relationship with God. Ron and Lisa grew in their relationship with God during a major period of transition and crisis. Later we will discover this to be a common pattern. The Apostle Paul wrote: ''. . . suffering produces perseverance; perseverance, character; and character, hope. And hope does not disappoint us, because God has poured out his love into our hearts by the Holy Spirit, whom he has given us'' (Rom. 5:3-5).

Christian growth is developmental much in the same way that adulthood is developmental (1 John 2:12-14). Our growth as Christians should affect how we respond to the developmental tasks and issues of adult life.

The Bible and the Structure of Life

The concept of life structure provides important insights related to how our lives develop and change over time. And naturally, for most people the goal is to make choices and commitments that lead to a more meaningful and fulfilled life. Mankind is engaged in a quest for meaning and its members attempt to invest their lives to achieve the greatest return. The developmental nature of our existence makes this a lifelong wager.

No single life structure is sufficient for the diverse tasks of adulthood. As long as one faces a future there are decisions to be made which will affect that future for better or for worse. It is at this point that we must listen carefully to what the biblical text has to say about those choices and about the structure of one's existence.

In a biblical sense, the building or modifying of one's life structure corresponds to the renewing of the mind. It is the process of ''putting off the old self'' and replacing it with the ''new self.'' Deceitful desires are to be replaced by righteousnes and holiness (Eph. 4:22-24).

While this process involves personal commitment and perseverance (Rom. 6:19), it is not, nor is it intended to be, an individual struggle for perfection. Christian transformation occurs within the context of the community of believers through mutual support and edification (Eph. 4:11-16).

Meaningful life is only possible where there are shared commitments. For example, when we receive our driver's license we agree to commit ourselves to the rules of the road. We recognize that a red light means stop and a green light means go. Everyone who is given a driver's license must share this same understanding. They must also be committed to the same rules that we are. Without this shared understanding and commitment driving would be dangerous and chaotic.

Christian growth can only occur when there are shared commitments. The biblical expression for this is covenant. Life is made up of covenants and without them we would be in a constant state of confusion. We make a covenant with the bank when we take out a loan, or with the landlord when we rent an apartment. We make covenants with clients and employers, with friends, with the government, with family members— our lives are embedded in covenant relationships. These covenants help to produce stability. They aid us in understanding what is expected of both us and others in specific settings and relationships. Sometimes these covenants are written down. Sometimes they are oral or can be found in traditions. Without them life would be without definition and direction. Covenants are critical in the development of a stable life structure.

Jesus Christ made an eternal covenant with us when he died on the cross. It is the New Covenant. It is binding upon those under the rule of God. This covenant gives definition to our lives as Christians. It redefines life in new terms which are set forth in the scriptures. If we are to fully embrace this new life, we must be willing to live within the demands that this covenant sets forth: to love God and to love one another.

Our covenant relationship with God is based on faith. This "faithful" relationship provides stability in coping with and responding to life. The glue which bonds the covenant together is God's love. Even if there are times when it seems as if we have no faith, God will remain faithful to us (2 Tim. 2:13). Nothing can separate us from his love (Rom. 8:38-39). This is the good news. The new covenant brings new life.

In order for the new covenant to become binding, we must accept its terms without negotiation. The terms are capsulized in Jesus' own proclamation, "The kingdom of God is near. Repent and believe the good news!" (Mark 1:15).

Jesus preached the need for repentance. While his message was similar to that of John the Baptist, at the heart of it there was an essential difference.[6] Repentance means a change in the direction of one's life. For the Jews this would have signified a new dedication to the law.

Obedience would replace disobedience. For Jesus, though, repentance meant something far more radical. It entailed a fundamental change in the direction of one's life. It implied a totally new existence in which one's entire life was redirected through a total change in perspective of one's self and the world. This could not be accomplished on a partial basis. It required total commitment; not to a new set of principles or laws, but to Jesus himself.

Jesus' message of repentance was yoked to his proclamation of good news concerning the Kingdom of God. We would misunderstand Jesus and the thrust of the New Testament if we were to place our major emphasis upon turning away from individual acts of sin. Though this is surely required, it misses the radical nature of conversion. What is required is not a new morality, but a total restructuring of life. Past commitments, relationships, values, and goals must be replaced by a whole new pattern and design for living.

In order to appreciate the need for total conversion, we must first comprehend the pervasive and destructive nature of sin. Individual acts of sin are conditioned by the comprehensive nature of sin and death which dominate all of creation. It is not enough to stop sinning. To fully experience life, one must be removed from this death-dominated sphere of existence. Jesus Christ has made this possible through his own death on the Cross (Gal. 1:3–4; Col. 1:13; Eph. 2:1–3). Deliverance implies a new freedom to embrace life and to experience its fulness. But such freedom must be continually embraced or one will quickly slip back into slavery.

Repentance requires a recognition that one's life is headed in the wrong direction. In order to experience salvation, we must first admit that we are powerless to alter our own life circumstances in any ultimate sense. No matter how hard we try or what we do, it will be insufficient to bring about fulness of life which every person earnestly seeks. Furthermore, our own efforts to secure life are not only inadequate, but they bring about further destruction, not only to ourselves, but to others as well. We cannot escape the penalty of sin—death.

For the Christian, this perspective is critical for understanding faith development throughout the stages of life. All human beings, whether they like it or not, experience transition periods in which their life structure is modified. This is true for both Christians and non-Christians. Yet mankind left to its own wisdom and insight cannot adequately provide for its own existence. It cannot develop a satisfactory life structure.

To experience life, there must be a surrender of one's will expressed through a total commitment to the person of Jesus Christ. Repentance paves the way for a radical change in the structure of one's existence. Repentance is not simply an act of confession, but a total conversion and redirection of one's life. If affects every aspect of one's life structure. Commitments, values, perceptions, relationships, and goals all become redefined in terms of a relationship with the living Christ.

The character of this relationship then becomes expressed and sustained through faith in the Son of God. The Christian's response to every challenge, opportunity, crisis, or change that emerges in the course of life is to reflect an unwavering commitment to Jesus himself.

Summary

The human life cycle is made up of several stages or eras. Within the adult years we can distinguish between early, middle, and later adulthood. Each stage can be subdivided into shorter developmental periods. These periods have their own developmental issues and tasks. The successful achievement of current tasks increases the likelihood of coping well with tasks later in life.

One important task during each stage is to build a stable life structure. Our life structure is reflected in our goals, choices, commitments, values, and relationships. Life space refers to the scope and complexity of our environment.

Life structures tend to shift as we experience transitions. Some transitions are predictable, but others come unexpectedly. We can expect transitions to occur throughout life. Transition periods may last four or five years. During these times we may ask important questions concerning who we are and where we are going in life. These may be difficult times, but they can also result in personal growth and development.

We each have an internal sense of timing, known as the social clock, which lets us know if we are "on-time" or "off-time" in our social and personal development. This sense of timing may speed us up or slow us down with respect to the achievement of personal goals.

As we move through the life cycle, certain events stand out as milestones. Milestones serve as important reference points as we consider where we have been and ponder where we are going in life.

As Christians, our faith in God makes a decisive and positive difference in how we respond to life changes or crises. Repentance paves the way for a new relationship with God through Jesus Christ resulting in a totally new existence. This relationship is based upon faith in the Son of God. Faith enables us to respond to difficult and seemingly impossible situations with a new source of strength and hope. It gives us a fresh perspective on life and a new understanding of who we are and who we are becoming. In faith we embrace the Eternal.

4
The Structure of Faith

Faith lies at the heart of Christian life. The writer of Hebrews instructs us that without faith it is impossible to please God (11:6). Faith has little to do with dogma or ritual. The true object of faith is Jesus Christ. To believe in the gospel is to believe in Jesus. Jesus said, ''Do not let your hearts be troubled. Trust in God; trust also in me'' (John 14:1). Belief in Jesus leads to eternal life (John 3:16). Those who do not believe in him live in darkness and experience judgment (John 3:18f.).

Recognizing the critical importance of faith, we must ask how faith fits into the total pattern or design of one's life. In the preceding chapter we discussed the concept of life structure, the basic pattern or design of a person's life. Values, relationships, goals, commitments, and perceptions concerning one's self and the world reflect life structure. Now we must examine the structure of faith. How is faith integrated into the life structure? How should faith be expressed in the way we live? If it is true that our life structure goes through alternating periods of stability and transition, what implications does that have, if any, for the expression of faith? Does our faith change in relationship to changes in our life structure? Or is faith the stablizing force in the midst of change? What part does and should faith play in the building and modifying of personal goals, commitments, relationships and values? In this chapter we will examine the biblical structure of faith and its relationship to the structure of life.

The Biblical Structure of Faith

At one time or another, most of us will take some complex aspect of life and see it as one-dimensional. We will ignore everything about that issue that we don't understand, that we disagree with, or that seems to threaten our perspective. The problem is that life is not one-dimensional. There is more to it than what we usually see from our limited vantage point. Faith is the same way.

Borrowing the illustration from H. Richard Niebuhr, James Fowler has noted that faith is like a cube.[1] Although a cube has six sides, it is only possible to see three sides at any one time. Different sides become visible as the cube is rotated. The same is true with faith. Certain aspects of faith always remain hidden from our sight. Yet they are still there. From a biblical perspective, faith is to be expressed in at least the following ways.[2]

Belief

One aspect of faith is belief in God's Word or message. This includes belief in both the scriptures (John 2:22; 5:46; Acts 24:14) and the preaching of the gospel (Eph. 1:13; 1 Cor. 1:21). Faith comes from hearing the Word of Christ (Rom. 10:17) and is to lead to the confession that Jesus is Lord (Rom. 10:8f.).

We would be mistaken to associate belief in the gospel to mental assent to a certain set of propositions. Faith has to do with the individual's total response to life. What a person believes or holds to be true must be translated into a total orientation toward life based upon God's saving deed in Christ. Faith, then, must be expressed in belief in the gospel. Belief in the gospel becomes evident in obedience to Christ. This leads us to the second dimension of faith.

Obedience

If faith in Christ is to have meaning, it must be translated into obedience. Like Abraham, the Christian is to express faith through obedience (Heb. 11:8f.). Faith in Jesus means a new orientation to life. Repentance requires a change in direction. Faith makes that change possible.

The new life is not based upon works or law although it is expected that good works will result from it (Eph. 2:8–10). It is a life of faith through which Jesus himself becomes our life (Gal. 2:20).

As an apostle, Paul viewed his own ministry as bringing "about the obedience of faith among all the Gentiles" (Rom. 1:15). This obedience of faith enables true obedience which the law had demanded, but which was impossible. This new obedience glorifies God as we live out our confession in tangible, practical ways (2 Cor. 9:13). Unbelief, on the other hand, leads to disobedience (Heb. 3:18–19).

Faith is not simply assent to the gospel, but rather an expression of commitment to a new way of life embodied in Jesus Christ. But this is not a cold, sterile relationship. It is of the most intimate nature based upon total trust.

Trust

The Christian is to no longer have confidence in his or her own power. Trust in God is to replace trust in one's self. Jesus solicits that trust (John 14:1). Dependency upon Christ is reflected in a total lack of boasting concerning our new life (1 Cor. 1:29, 31). The new life comes from Christ (1 Cor. 1:30), apart from whom we have no ability to change our life circumstances (1 Cor. 4:7).

Abraham and Sarah exemplify trust in God. Sarah received the ability to conceive through faith. This faith was possible because she considered God to be faithful (Heb. 11:11). Likewise, Abraham grew strong in faith because he believed the promise of God that Sarah would conceive (Rom. 4:19f.). They both trusted God.

When we trust someone, we place confidence in what they say or do. When we trust God it means that our confidence must be in him. What he says is all that matters. Paul reflected this attitude. On his trip to Rome, Paul and his sailing companions encountered a violent storm. The sailors became convinced that all would be lost, even their own lives. An angel appeared to Paul revealing to him that no one would perish. Paul encouraged the crew and travelers with the following word: ". . . keep up your courage, men, for I have faith in God that it will happen just as he told me" (Acts 27:25).

Faith cannot survive without the dimension of trust. Trust proclaims, "God is faithful. He will do what he says." The scriptures instruct us, "if we are faithless, he will remain faithful" (2 Tim. 2:13). God will not break his Word. This leads us to the next dimension—faithfulness.

Faithfulness

The same act of faith that receives new life also demands that we remain faithful to the Christ who redeemed us. Faith is not an experience or a general attitude or disposition concerning life. Rather, it is an ongoing, dynamic relationship with the Son of God that alters every facet of our existence. Everything becomes new (2 Cor. 5:17).

In this new relationship we are saved by grace (Eph. 2:8). We also become stewards or caretakers of the grace of God (1 Pet. 4:10). As servants of Christ and stewards of God's grace, we are to be found trustworthy or faithful (1 Cor. 4:1–2). Faithfulness continually renews life. Unfaithfulness, on the other hand, brings about death and destruction.

Hope

A fifth dimension of faith is hope. Faith in God points to the future. "Salvation is nearer now than when we first believed" (Rom. 13:11). Faith contains an element of anticipation (1 Thess. 4:13ff.). By faith we await the hope of righteousness (Gal. 5:5). Yet at the same time faith makes salvation real now. We are the children of God. What we will be is hidden from our sight, but we will become like Jesus (1 John 3:2; Col. 3:1–4; Phil. 3:20f.). This is the Christian hope and through it we were saved (Rom. 8:24).

Without hope freedom becomes impossible. Hope frees the believer to totally trust God. Anxieties about the future are no longer to haunt the Christian. The future is secure in Christ who provides an anchor for the soul (Heb. 6:19).

The unbeliever must compete against an unknown future. He or she becomes dependent upon personal resources and struggles to secure existence through individual efforts. Yet the end result is always the same—death. Death becomes the one future reality which is guaranteed.

Jesus said, "For whoever wants to save his life will lose it, but whoever loses his life for me will save it" (Luke 9:24). This is the paradox of faith. Those who attempt to secure their future through their own means will become consumed by that future. The only fruit will be fear, anxiety, striving, and ultimately death.

Faith, on the other hand, expresses trust in Jesus and hope for the future. Rather than seeking to preserve one's life, faith leads to the seeking of the Kingdom of God (Matt. 6:33). God's rule replaces our rule, and our lives become his life (Gal. 2:20).

Those with such hope embark on a new journey. The Christian is to be a pilgrim, a stranger, an exile, a sojourner in a foreign land. Faith becomes revealed in a steadfast conviction that there is another land with a city whose builder and maker is God. Faith reveals another dimension to life (Heb. 11:1). Through faith, we embrace everlasting life and welcome the promises of God from a distance (Heb. 11:13).

Faith and the Structure of Life

As we have seen above, faith is multi-dimensional. From a biblical perspective, *belief, trust, obedience, faithfulness,* and *hope* are all expressions of faith. Yet faith cannot be reduced to these dimensions alone. As we have noted, faith is not a virtue, a moral characteristic, an attitude, a disposition, or some magical power; rather, faith characterizes the fabric of one's existence. For the Christian, faith is a manifestation of one's relationship with God. It is not simply an aspect of one's life structure; faith becomes the foundational structure of life. Every commitment, goal, value, or relationship becomes an expression of faith in Jesus Christ. Faith is at the center of Christian existence. It shapes every other aspect of life and is to be most clearly expressed through love (Gal 5:6). Ultimately, only love alone matters. Faith, hope, and love will endure forever (1 Cor. 13:13). Faith, therefore, is not passive, but is actively expressed in how one engages life. Faith without works is dead (James 2:17f.).

We are now faced with the question of how faith is expressed in practice. To what extent are the biblical dimensions of faith such as belief, obedience, trust, faithfulness, and hope expressed in the lives of Christians? Do other expressions of faith emerge? And finally, how do the various expressions of faith develop and change?

5

The Expression of Faith

Looking back over his life, the Apostle Paul reflected, "I have fought the good fight, I have finished the race, I have kept the faith" (2 Tim. 4:7). From the moment that Paul encountered Jesus Christ on the road to Damascus to his imprisonment in Rome and eventual execution, his life became directed and sustained by faith in the living Christ (Gal. 2:20). Thus Paul challenged his converts to walk even as he had walked (Phil. 3:17). This way of life included a reaching forward to spiritual growth, a pressing on toward perfection. All Christians were to have this attitude (Phil. 3:12-15).

On various occasions, Paul was concerned that believers were slipping back into patterns of life that thwarted spiritual growth (Gal. 4:11). The writer of Hebrews confronted Christians who regressed in their faith. By the time they should have been teachers of God's word, they were in need of elementary instruction themselves (Heb. 5:12f.). The biblical writers expected Christians to mature in their faith (2 Pet. 1:5-11). This maturity was to be an expression of the dynamic power of God in the life of the believer. While Christians who were young in the faith knew the joy of sins forgiven, they would eventually experience the struggles of spiritual warfare (Eph. 6:11ff.). However, it was expected that they would overcome the evil one and live a victorious life (1 John 2:14).

The life of faith is a dynamic journey. Like Abraham, we are engaged in a quest that is sustained by faith in God. The scriptures teach us that faith in God is to mature with time. It is not enough to have faith, knowledge, self-control, or other expressions of Christian life. In order to remain effective servants of Christ, these qualities must be increasing and continually practiced (2 Pet. 1:5ff.).

In practice, how is faith in God expressed, and how does that expression of faith change over time? Until recently, little attention had been given to these questions. Contemporary research is beginning to shed some light on these concerns.

Stages of Faith

James Fowler has recently suggested that there are six distinct and progressive stages of faith.[1] However, few people experience all six stages. According to Fowler, all human beings have faith in something. Faith does not have to be religious in nature; rather, it can be oriented towards power, money, people, or whatever. Faith serves to integrate life in such a way as to give one purpose, meaning, and direction. It shapes the way we invest our lives. Faith is not simply belief in propositional statements, but is an orientation to life.

Each of Fowler's six stages represents a new development in how faith is expressed. Stage one is most common between the ages of three and seven. Lacking the ability to think logically, the young child experiences faith through imagination. This stage is characterized by fantasy and imitation. Long-lasting feelings and images are constructed that will influence future faith development.

The second stage begins around age seven. During this period the child develops a more personal faith. Stories play a powerful role in both the development and expression of faith.

Stage three emerges as the child (or in some cases the adult) begins to reflect on the social and interpersonal implications of the stories. This would tend to occur as the individual's world begins to extend beyond the boundaries of the family. As the environment becomes more complex, faith helps to synthesize values and plays a role in the formation of personal identity.

Stages four through six are not experienced by all adults. Most individuals, however, would enter stage four during late adolescence or early adulthood. Stage four is marked by personal responsibility and the differentiation of one's own beliefs and outlook from those of others. Stage five strives to unify conflicting experiences and world views in both mind and practice. Truth becomes revealed in both paradoxes and apparent contradictions. Finally, stage six, which few actually experience, is the culminating image of mature faith. From one perspective it is the incarnation of absolute love and justice. For the Christian, this is embodied in the coming Kingdom of God.

Fowler's study deserves careful attention. He raises many important issues related to faith. Whether or not faith actually develops in stages, is still questionable, especially during the adult years; however, there does appear to be a definite relationship between faith development and developmental issues and tasks associated with particular periods of life. That relationship will be the primary focus of the remainder of this book.

From a biblical perspective, it is questionable whether or not Fowler's discussion of faith does justice to what it means to have faith in Christ as opposed to any other form of faith. His conception of faith as a unifying principle of life is similar to what sociologists Peter Berger and Thomas Luckmann have described as a symbolic universe.[2] Every individual faces the need to organize his or her perception of life in such a way as to give it meaning and direction. Something has to hold our perception of reality together. The symbolic universe serves this function. It organizes everyday roles and priorities by placing them within a broader context of meaning. For example, for the Christian the rule of God provides a perspective which is to unify life and give direction and substance to both values and decisions.

Various conceptual approaches are used in the development and maintenance of a symbolic universe. For example, science, theology, mythology, or philosophy can be used to frame and structure reality. In Western societies, science has become the dominant medium used to interpret and understand the world.

To some degree faith serves this function for Fowler. Since faith is not necessarily religious, it can take on the shape and color of any of these conceptual approaches. Among other things faith can be scientific, political, mythological, or theological in its orientation. One must ask, however, how faith in Christ is different from faith in anything else.

Leonhard Goppelt has noted that Jesus was unique in the way he spoke of faith.[3] According to Goppelt, the Hellenistic world at the time of Christ did not solicit faith toward any deity. Even for the Jews, the normative expression of faith was obedience to the law. Faith was a work under other works.

The expression, "Your faith has saved you," originated with Jesus. For Jesus faith was necessary for salvation. In addition, Goppelt has indicated that the content of such faith was nothing less than a personal investment in Jesus, not as a miracle-worker, but as the Son of God. Those who responded to Jesus placed their trust and confidence in him. Furthermore, faith was reflected in repentance whereby a person turned away from his or her own self and turned to God. In actuality that meant placing trust in Jesus (John 14:1). According to John that is the normative expression of faith.

From a biblical perspective, everything that directs or shapes existence apart from God is idolatry. For the Christian, life becomes defined totally in terms of one's relationship with Jesus Christ. Jesus' message is to repent and believe the good news. This message is normative for the development of genuine faith as well as its expression. Those who would follow Jesus Christ must accept his Lordship. It means nothing less than total commitment to Christ.

Faith leads to life only when the object of that faith is the Son of God. Such faith is to be expressed through love in acts of obedience to and trust in a living Lord and Savior, Jesus Christ. Furthermore, faith is sustained by hope in the future reign of Christ. Faith expressed in these terms is more than a conceptual integration of reality. Faith becomes the very fabric which sustains life. Every other form of faith sustains life only at the ultimate cost of death.

For Fowler, a person always has faith in something. This indeed may be true. The question still remains, however, how does the Christian's "faith" differ from any other kind of "faith?" This becomes a critical question when discussing Fowler's stage six, the incarnation of love and justice. Can ultimate love and justice be found apart from Christ himself? And can it be expressed apart from faith in the Son of God?

Jesus' call for repentance places a radical demand upon the individual. Repentance leads to a new life, not to a reformed life. Conversion is more than replacing ultimate symbols of meaning with different symbols of meaning; rather, it is an encounter with the living Christ that totally recreates one's existence. It is not simply a change in orientation or in the way we perceive life, although that is to occur (Rom. 12:2); conversion brings about regeneration. It is a spiritual experience that defies explanation in purely psychological or phenomenological terms.

The radical nature of Christian conversion and the uniqueness of faith in Christ is an issue requiring further discussion. From a New Testament perspective faith in Christ is viewed as unique for it alone leads to salvation. The focus of this study was to examine and portray various ways that faith in Christ is expressed throughout different periods of the life cycle.

Faith Responses

How is faith in God expressed during the adult years? As we have already mentioned, for the Christian, faith is to be reflected in the very fabric of one's life. It becomes an expression of the individual's relationship with God. Faith activates a spiritual regeneration that transforms one's existence.

This study examined the more prominent ways that faith in God is actually expressed. Two different approaches were used to collect information. First, in-depth interviews were held with forty-seven men and thirty-six women ranging in age from eighteen to eighty-one. Age-wise, these individuals were evenly distributed over the life cycle. Second, based on interview findings, a questionnaire was designed and distributed to an additional 265 adults.

Faith in God tended to be expressed in a variety of ways depending upon the individual's age, life circumstances, background, and relationship to God. In total, twenty-two different faith responses emerged during the interviews. These responses are listed below:

1. God meets my needs
2. Trust in God
3. The Bible
4. Seeking direction from God
5. Reason to live
6. Reliance upon the sustaining power of God
7. Serving, using my gifts
8. Personal relationship
9. Sensing God's presence
10. Hope
11. Life perspective
12. Prayer
13. Moralistic, concerns about right and wrong
14. Assurance

15. More content with life
16. Becoming whole
17. More accepting, less dogmatic
18. Trust in myself
19. Power over evil
20. Avoiding hell
21. Relying more on others
22. Intellectual concerns

Each individual developed his or her own repertoire of faith responses. Within the repertoire, a particular cluster of responses emerged in importance. This cluster tends to change over time, either expanding or contracting in size. While certain responses persist over time, others tend to wax and wane. For example, while an intellectual approach to faith may be important in early adulthood; it may disappear later in life. However, faith responses cannot be turned on and off like a light switch. Rather, they are expressions of the individual's relationship with God. As that relationship changes, the expression of faith tends to change as well.

A particular cluster of responses may be prominent for an extended period of time. As the individual moves through various developmental periods, this cluster may undergo change. While particular faith responses may persist, others may become less important.

There appeared to be some correlation between faith responses and developmental tasks associated with particular periods of the life cycle. That is, there does appear to be some predictable issues that arise throughout life that affect the development of faith. These relationships will be discussed more fully in the remaining chapters.

The following four faith responses tended to be the most prominent for both men and women: (1) God meets my needs; (2) Trust in God; (3) the Bible; and, (4) Seeking direction. It is noteworthy that nearly all of the responses focused on personal issues and concerns. Few individuals connected faith development to issues related to the corporate or social structures of life. That is not to say that no connections existed. When given the opportunity to share about their own development and expression of faith, personal issues and concerns dominated. (Tables I, II and III, which are based upon questionnaire findings, provide a more comprehensive portrayal of the various faith responses related to the age and gender of the respondents.)

TABLE I

FAITH RESPONSES: MEN

Total Number of Respondents (N) = 90

M: Indicates a response expressed by at least one-third of the respondents

Number Age	N=11 18–23	N=10 24–27	N=16 28–33	N=12 34–37	N=13 38–43	N=9 44–47	N=10 48–53	N=5 54–64	N=4 65–up
1. God meets needs	M	M	M	M	M	M	M	M	M
2. Trust in God		M	M		M	M	M	M	
3. The Bible		M		M	M	M	M	M	M
4. Seeking direction	M		M			M			
5. Reason to live				M		M	M		
6. Serving	M	M		M		M			
7. Personal relation				M					M
8. God's presence							M		M
9. Hope	M								M
10. Life perspective					M	M	M		
11. Assurance									M
12. More accepting							M		

The following observations are relevant concerning the above responses:

1. Believing that God would meet personal needs was the most frequent expression of faith among men.

2. Placing one's trust in God and reading the Bible were important expressions of faith for most age groups.

3. Seeking direction from God was an important response in early adulthood and tended to surface during transition periods. For example, forty-five percent of the men between eighteen and twenty-three and thirty-seven percent of those between twenty-eight and thirty-three did not feel that they had a clear sense of direction from God. Discerning the will of God was often related to finding a job, changing careers, or in trying to become reoriented after a divorce or some other personal loss.

4. Men tended to view faith in God as providing a perspective on life more frequently during middle age. This may be due to increased personal reflection concerning life direction which often occurs during the forties.

5. It should also be noted according to the interview findings that intellectual concerns related to faith in God were found, for the most part, only during early adulthood. They tended to surface most frequently during the late teens and early twenties and declined with age.

TABLE II

Faith Responses: Women

Total Number of Respondents (N) = 175

W: Indicates a response expressed by at least one-third of the respondents

Number	N=15	N=20	N=36	N=23	N=24	N=16	N=16	N=15	N=10
Age	18–23	24–27	28–33	34–37	38–43	44–47	48–53	54–64	65–up
1. God meets needs	W	W	W	W	W	W	W	W	W
2. Trust in God	W	W	W	W	W	W	W	W	W
3. The Bible	W	W	W		W	W	W	W	W
4. Seeking direction	W	W		W	W	W		W	
5. Reason to live		W				W	W	W	W
6. Sustaining power					W	W	W	W	W
7. Serving		W	W	W					
8. Personal relation	W	W	W	W					
9. God's presence				W		W		W	W
10. Hope					W			W	
11. Life perspective							W	W	
12. Prayer							W		W
13. Moralistic									W
14. Assurance								W	

The following observations are relevant concerning the above responses:

1. The three responses of God meets my needs, trust in God and reading the Bible were the most common expressions of faith among women.

2. Seeking God's will was a significant response across the life cycle for women. On the average, one-third of the respondents were seeking direction from God. This was especially true for women between the ages of thirty-four and forty-three and fifty-four to sixty-four where nearly fifty percent were uncertain concerning their life direction. Over fifty-five percent of the women between thirty-four and forty-three felt that their life was in the midst of change. In general, this was true for thirty to forty percent of all women except those over age sixty-five who felt more stable.

3. Beginning with the transition into middle age (thirty-eight to forty-three), reliance upon the sustaining power of God became an important response and continued throughout the remainder of the life cycle. Interview findings indicated that this was true for women earlier in life

as well. This faith response was frequently associated with coping with problems, stress or crises.

4. Faith as a personal relationship with God was important in early adulthood, but became less prominent later in life. Yet an awareness of God's presence tended to surface in middle and later adulthood.

5. The overall cluster of faith responses expanded slightly later in life.

TABLE III

FAITH RESPONSES AS A PERCENTAGE OF THE TOTAL

Total Number of Respondents (N) = 265

Total Number Group	N=90 % Men	N=175 % Women	N=265 % Combined
1. God meets needs	51%	49%	51%
2. Trust in God	46	50	48
3. The Bible	47	44	45
4. Seeking direction	31	35	34
5. Reason to live	27	34	32
6. Sustaining power	24	35	31
7. Serving	31	31	31
8. Personal relation	26	32	30
9. God's presence	18	33	28
10. Hope	27	27	27
11. Life perspective	30	23	26
12. Prayer	12	27	22
13. Moralistic	21	18	19
14. Assurance	16	17	17
15. More content	17	9	11
16. Becoming whole	9	11	10
17. More accepting	11	10	10
18. Trust in myself	13	7	9
19. Power over evil	7	9	8
20. Avoiding hell	3	10	8
21. Relying on others	3	3	3
22. Intellectual concerns	3	1	2

A comparison between the faith responses of men and women reveals the following:

1. The responses of God meets my needs, trust in God and reading the Bible were the most common expressions of faith for both men and women.

2. The transition into adulthood was characterized by seeking direction from God by both men and women. The age thirty transition and the decade of the forties also surfaced as important directional seeking periods for men. The forties was also characterized by men as a period to view faith as providing a perspective on life. Women, on the other hand, felt that their lives were in the midst of change much more frequently than did men. The period from ages thirty-four to forty-three appeared to be the most turbulent time for women. This may be due to significant role changes related to both child rearing and career. These findings are illustrated more clearly in the table below.

TABLE IV

CONCERNS RELATED TO LIFE DIRECTION

Total Number of Respondents (N) = 275

Number of Men	N=11	N=10	N=16	N=12	N=13	N=9	N=10	N=5	N=4
Number of Women	N=15	N=20	N=36	N=23	N=24	N=16	N=16	N=15	N=10
Age	18–23	24–27	28–33	34–37	38–43	44–47	48–53	54–64	65–up
1. Faith seeking direction									
A. Men	73%	10%	44%	25%	31%	33%	20%	—	—
B. Women	53%	40%	28%	39%	33%	38%	25%	40%	30%
2. Unclear concerning God's will									
A. Men	45%	30%	37%	33%	23%	23%	20%	—	—
B. Women	33%	25%	28%	48%	46%	12%	31%	47%	30%
3. Feeling that one's life is in the midst of change									
A. Men	73%	20%	31%	17%	46%	44%	—	20%	—
B. Women	40%	40%	36%	74%	37%	37%	44%	40%	10%

3. Reliance upon the sustaining power of God was a significant faith response for women from ages thirty-eight on. However, this expression of faith did not appear to be as important to men.

4. During middle age, both men and women were more likely to express faith in God as providing a reason to live. This may be due to the stripping away of illusions which are more prominent in early adulthood.

5. In general, the cluster of prominent faith responses tended to expand in number for both men and women from middle age on.

It should be emphasized that the above findings represent the expression of faith in a generalized way for the group which was studied. Each individual develops his or her own unique repertoire of faith responses. Within any particular period of life, a cluster of responses will emerge in importance. However, this cluster expands and contracts over time as life issues and personal circumstances change. For example, faith seeking direction may emerge as a prominent response during times of transition, but then may rapidly decline in importance once directional issues become clarified. On the other hand, certain faith responses tend to provide stability and are more likely to persist over time. One such response is believing that "God will meet my needs." For some this may be thought of in a selfish or self-serving way, but for most individuals it is a more specific expression of trust as illustrated in Paul's letter to the Philippians: "And my God will meet all your needs according to his glorious riches in Christ Jesus" (4:19). In a more generalized sense, trust in God also served as a stablizing expression of faith. It expressed confidence or reliance upon a faithful God. God is considered trustworthy. He will do what he says. More specifically, such trust was related to the Bible. Trust in the Bible was a third stablizing expression of faith.

For most individuals, these three expressions of faith (or similar responses) became the pillars for a stable Christian life. Most of the other faith responses were more likely to wax or wane depending upon particular life circumstances. These three, however, tended to persist over time. For most, the expression of faith was closely tied to an individual pilgrimage. While other individuals often played a key role in the development of faith, the expression of faith was generally associated with individual actions and commitments rather than being viewed as part of a community of believers. Little connection was made between faith and the power structures of modern life.

Faith and Power

Faith in God and the power of the Holy Spirit enable the Christian to respond to life differently than the non-believer. How we respond to life is not simply a question of perception or world view, but also of power. Jesus had power to forgive sins (Matt. 9:6); to heal sicknesses (Mark 3:15); to cast out unclean spirits (Mark 6:7). He spoke with such power that those who heard him were astonished (Luke 4:22). In fact, all power has been given to him both in heaven and on earth (Matt. 28:18).

Jesus has given us power to become the children of God (John 1:12). The gospel is the power of God for the salvation of everyone who believes (Rom. 1:16). Those who receive the Holy Spirit are endued with power to testify of the saving act of Jesus Christ (Acts 1:8).

The Holy Spirit empowers the Christian to lead a victorious life. We are more than conquerors through him who loved us (Rom. 8:37). He who is in us is greater than the one who is in the world (1 John 4:4). Nor will God abandon us. Nothing can separate us from the love of God (Rom. 8:39). We can be confident that he who began a good work in us will complete it (Phil. 1:6). And furthermore, no life circumstance is too overwhelming. We can do everything through him who gives us strength (Phil. 4:13).

Faith is to be translated into power—power that testifies of God's redeeming grace. It is power over death; power over the demonic; power to heal; power to love; power to endure; power to serve; power to live free from the cares of life; power to be content in any circumstance. Yet it is not personal power. Such power is present only when we surrender our own will and respond in obedience to the will of God. His power in our lives is the strongest when we are the weakest.

Faith in God and the power of the Holy Spirit are inseparable. One cannot exist without the other. Unfortunately, though, some attempt to translate faith into magical power. Faith becomes reduced to a formula. Faith becomes a means to manipulate God, who is turned into a vending machine. This is not Christian faith, but a ''faith'' that is used to legitimize greed. Its primary focus is self-serving.

Such faith is contrary to the nature of Christ. Jesus did not entrust himself to those who believed in him because of his miracles. He knew what was in man (John 2:23ff.). God responds to those with a contrite heart (Isa. 57:15). The true power of faith is seen in the one who follows in the footsteps of Jesus; who gives up life in order that it may be found; who does not boast, but whose only glory is in the Cross of Christ.

Christian faith is unique because it alone brings salvation. The just shall live by faith—faith in the Son of God who loved us and gave his life for us. However faith is expressed, it is to glorify God and point to Jesus as the Pioneer and Perfecter of our faith (Heb. 12:2).

Summary

Faith in God is to mature with time. The biblical writers expected Christians to press on toward perfection. The way we express faith seems to be affected by important developmental issues that are associated with various stages of life. While no two individuals express faith in exactly the same way, certain faith responses tend to be more prominent than others. Some like believing that God will meet *my* needs, trust in God and reading the Bible were the three most common expressions of faith discovered in this study. Other important faith responses surfaced as well.

Faith in God is a source of power for the Christian. It is not personal power, but power to live a victorious life that glorifies God. This does not mean that the Christian is free from life difficulties; but rather, through faith in Christ the Christian is strengthened to face any situation or circumstance.

Some individuals attempt to use faith to manipulate God. This is not Christian faith. Authentic faith trusts in God. It is not self-serving.

In the following chapters we will focus upon the expression and development of faith within various developmental periods. Particular attention will be given to the changing nature of faith responses as we move through the stages of life.

6
The Transition into Adulthood

The transition period leading into adulthood begins at about age seventeen and lasts around five years. This is a period filled with important decisions and rapidly changing roles, relationships, and responsibilities. Two important tasks which characterize this transition are leaving one's family and settling into a more stable pattern of life as a young adult.

This process includes two primary tasks related to the expression of faith. The first is to establish a basis for faith apart from what one's parents or other authority figures believe. The second is to begin to clarify what one believes to be God's will for his or her life.

In this chapter we are going to examine the transitional experience of three young adults as they enter the adult world. While each individual's experience is unique, nevertheless, themes emerge which are played out in the lives of countless others. These themes included the search for identity, the establishment of values, leaving one's parents, concerns for the future, and rethinking one's faith in God.

Sarah Dobbins, Age Twenty-one

Sarah Dobbins was a small-framed young woman with light brown hair down past her shoulders. She remembered making an important decision at the age of five. While she was attending Sunday school at the Methodist church, the teacher spoke to her about heaven and hell. Sarah recalled becoming a Christian at that time: "It was a practical decision. I didn't want to go to hell."

Sarah characterized her childhood by being a "good little girl" and always attending church with her parents. During junior high school she became involved with Youth for Christ. During that time family problems also began to surface. Her older sister Jane started using drugs and alcohol. On several occasions, Jane ran away from home. Finally, at age seventeen she became pregnant. Sarah was then thirteen years old.

In their attempt to cope with Jane, Sarah's parents sought spiritual help. Ultimately, this led them to a new church where they became involved in the charismatic movement. After what had happened to Jane, Sarah felt increased pressure not to disappoint her parents. Nevertheless, she felt uncomfortable in the new church and didn't feel that she fit into the youth group. She found herself more involved with groups outside of that church, especially with Campus Life.

After she graduated from high school, Sarah briefly attended a junior college and worked as a volunteer with Youth for Christ. However, she soon felt the need to be more on her own. This led her to leave home and to enroll in a Christian liberal arts college about 100 miles away from where her parents lived. It was during that time that Sarah began to reexamine her faith in God.

"There is a stage in life where you stop leaning on your parent's faith and develop your own. That's what I went through at college. I had a lot of questions on certain issues. I was always taught that things were a certain way, but now I don't always agree. I now disagree with my parents on certain issues which before I had always believed without questioning them."

Two years after moving away from home Sarah got married. That intensified the change process.

"Getting married changed my perspective on life. It wasn't just me anymore. I realized that what I did affected another person. In some ways I had to clean up my act. After we got married there were a lot of changes."

Immediately after the wedding, Sarah and her husband Dave moved to a small town several hours away from where her parents lived. There Dave, who had just graduated from college began a new job. Sarah, on the other hand, had to quit school early. At first she found the move difficult to accept and did not want to come. She was concerned about living in a small town as well as having to quit school. She finally resolved the issue.

"I realized I couldn't go my own way. Dave's career was more important. I was bothered at first, but now I've made new friends."

Eventually Sarah enrolled at a nearby college to finish her degree. While she and Dave planned to wait awhile to have children, she would not have been disappointed if she became pregnant. She dreamed about going to graduate school, but she was not sure if it would ever happen. In the meantime, they have discussed buying a house. The financial commitment scared Sarah.

When asked to describe how her faith had changed sinced her childhood and adolescent years, Sarah commented, "From accepting everything my minister and parents told me. Now I question it. I test it. I no longer rest on my parent's faith. I have my own—my own values, ideas, beliefs and concerns. I'm better grounded now as a Christian than I was before."

Sarah's transition into the adult world went fairly smoothly. Leaving her parent's home, getting married, becoming established in a home of her own, and developing her own faith all occurred without any major trauma. That is not to say that there was not some stress, however. Not everyone experiences such a smooth transition; Tony Sampson found the transition into adulthood to be a costly and painful experience, yet one with rewards as well.

Tony Sampson, Age Twenty-one

Tony Sampson was born in 1961 in Bloomington, Illinois. He was the middle child having an older and a younger sister. A major event occurred in his life in 1971 when his parents were divorced. A week after the divorce took place, his mother's parents came to visit and to everyone's shock his grandfather suddenly became ill and died.

His mother decided that she and the children should move to Phoenix and stay with her mother. Just a year and a half after the move Tony's grandmother died and the family moved back to Bloomington. Shortly after they returned, his mother began to date. Tony commented, "I wasn't naive about girls so that was an awkward time." Several years later she remarried. Tony got along well with his stepfather. He said, "Stepparents want to be accepted, but don't have that full authority. We weren't disciplined very much."

At age sixteen, however, Tony's world began to fall apart.

"My dad died when I was sixteen. His dad had died when he was sixteen. The security of being part of a family and then seeing it all fall apart—it was hard on me and made me less dependent and more independent. Since I was the only male, I had to be the man of the home.

"I didn't know it while he was alive, but my father was an alcoholic. That was the hardest thing for me to deal with in my life. The divorce didn't take him away, but then the death. My father and I were very close. He never told me he was dying, but he would give hints. He would say, 'Tony, I've taken care of you.' That was a very trying experience."

As Tony entered the adult world, his life became more turbulent and his quest for faith more intense.

"After father died, I felt I needed something—security. It was a rough period. I started to use drugs and began drinking a bit. That's not what I wanted though.

"I knew the Christian life was what I wanted. As a child I went to church but it didn't mean much to me. I never really experienced a relationship with God that affected everyday life. I just learned cold facts.

"I was a senior in high school and began to feel more independent. You have to make decisions on your own. I thought about faith, but I didn't let it rule my life.

"I started college and after three semesters I dropped out and got a job as a bartender. I was into drugs like marijuana and cocaine. All this time I still felt like I had some faith.

"I became dependent upon the drugs but they didn't solve any problems. I was having trouble coping with my father's death. Why did it have to happen? I didn't know he was an alcoholic until later and that was a rude awakening.

"I started seeing a psychologist. Even though I had a lot of friends, I didn't feel I could discuss these problems. Keeping all this inside really hurt. I was at the bottom of the pit. I didn't have anywhere else to go but up."

It was during that time that Tony found new faith in Christ.

"There wasn't a miraculous change. It took time to get guidance. I still didn't know what I wanted to do in school. It made it hard."

Tony's faith led to some practical decisions and new commitments in his life.

"I had been a bartender so I quit the job. I got a different job working as a landscaper. I also moved out of the fraternity. That was hard because

I had such a close relationship with so many of the guys. I needed to have my own space, to have more personal privacy. I needed time to think.

"Since I've recommitted my life to Christ, I feel more direction in my life now. I try to keep my commitment to God in perspective when I make a decision. I feel a second strength, an inner strength in tackling problems. I'm more interested in the Bible."

Tony's faith became strengthened when he prayed about a job and was then hired. While Tony felt much better about his life, he still sensed he had a long way to go. He was happier, though, with where his life was headed. Tony still had some problems with drugs but he believed God was helping him. He still faced major concerns related to his career and the possibility of marriage.

Tony's faith development was less related to an intellectual struggle and more a reflection of God's sustaining power. Tony needed help in coping with his problems. His faith provided an inner strength, yet at the same time he was trying to define what he believed. He needed time to think. He was unsure of what to study at college and was just beginning to read the Bible. Tony's faith commitment provided a new orientation in making decisions. And he was discovering that many decisions were yet to be made. In our next example Larry Griffin had arrived at a point in his life where he was about to make a pivotal decision. It would affect both his faith and his future for years to come.

Larry Griffin, Age Twenty-four

Larry Griffin was born in Boise, Idaho and grew up in a Christian home. The son of a Southern Baptist minister, he was regularly involved in church throughout his childhood and adolescence.

When Larry was fourteen, his family moved to Eugene, Oregon. His first job was working at a hamburger stand when he was eighteen, while he also attended junior college. During that time he continued to live at home with his parents.

When he was twenty, Larry experienced a major transition when he left home to attend college in southern California.

"That was a big step for me, moving away from home. That was the first time I had really gotten out from under my parents. I realized I was on my own. I didn't always have someone to turn to. Since my father was a minister, I always had to go to church and to do this and that.

But at college, I had to decide if there was anything to Christianity.''

At first Larry had a difficult time. He lived in a dorm and shared a room with four other students. He felt like he was the ''fifth wheel.'' The other four would do things together and leave him out. Larry felt unwanted and alone. He saw the situation as hopeless.

In frustration, he shared his feelings with a friend who was a Christian. She said, ''Let's pray and wait one week to see what happens.'' The situation began to improve and Larry felt that God had answered his prayer. ''It demonstrated the reality of God and the power of prayer.'' Through this experience Larry found a new group of Christian friends. ''By being with them I learned what it meant to be a Christian.''

A new test came after graduation when Larry moved to the Midwest to attend graduate school. For the first time in his life he felt truly independent. He pointed to a recent trip he had taken by himself to Canada and down the East Coast. Having fewer Christian friends at the new school, he felt like his faith now had to ''stand alone.'' He was at that time facing a critical decision concerning marriage.

''Last fall I developed a close relationship with a girl. It's really been good. Right now Ann is in Europe and she won't be back until this fall. I'm concerned though because she's not a Christian. I think a lot about her and about God. I'm trying to decide how to best communicate my beliefs to her.''

While Larry viewed the relationship as good, it had also become a major source of concern to him. Ann had become one of the most significant persons in his life. Yet she was not a Christian. He felt like the most important task in his life at that moment was to see her develop faith in Christ. Larry was also thinking about his career and wanted to get established in a job. His transition into adulthood was for the most part complete, but several important decisions were yet to be made.

In reviewing the development of his faith up to that point in his life, Larry made the following observations.

''The biggest change in my faith was going from the beliefs of my parents to be grounded in myself. It happened as I gained independence. When I was younger I thought of God as laying down a set of rules or guidelines to live by. If you abided by those guidelines, that was good enough. Toward the end of high school I became restless just doing things because I thought I had to. When I got to college I discovered more of a personal relationship. The change was from obeying rules imposed from the outside to delighting in the Lord.

"I've been struggling more with my faith of late. Mostly its just developing a constancy of belief. There are times when you feel God's presence—then it's easy to believe. There are other times when you're away from other Christians—then it takes faith, a constancy of belief to keep going. You may not feel that God is close, but he's still there if you need him."

Faith and the Transition into Adulthood

For Sarah, Tony, and Larry, the separation from their parents was a critical time for the establishment of their own belief in God. Sarah and Larry, who were both reared in Christian homes, found it a time to explore their own faith apart from that of their parents. Tony's faith was prompted by an intense search for meaning and security. For all three, belief in God became more of a personal reality instead of a list of rules to be obeyed or a set of cold facts to be learned.

Sarah, who married at age twenty, experienced the transition into adulthood without any major turbulence. The supportive environment of a Christian college, a dedicated Christian husband, and the establishment of a new home life brought about a sense of purpose and fulfillment. Sarah set aside her own career goals to support her husband's career. Although she was not planning to get pregnant, the unexpected did occur and she became an expectant mother.

For Tony, the transition into the adult world only intensified the turbulence that he had experienced as a child and adolescent. His parents' divorce, subsequently followed by the death of his father, propelled him into a quest to discover his own identity and purpose for living. Drugs and alcohol only complicated his problems.

While growing up, Tony had no real concept of faith even though he attended church. In the midst of despair he turned to God looking for help. His commitment of faith gave him a new sense of purpose. At the age of twenty-one, Tony's life was still highly unsettled. Feeling like he had just emerged from a dark pit, Tony was beginning to examine the options that faced him as an adult. He was beginning to explore life as a Christian, a new way of life which was still being defined.

Like Sarah, Larry renegotiated his faith once he left home. Attending a secular college, at first he found little support for his life as a Christian. Feeling personally rejected by his roommates, he felt lonely and depressed. The turning point came through the personal encouragement of another Christian and later by involvement in a Christian fellowship on campus. This helped prepare him later when he left to go to graduate school and felt more isolated as a Christian. Larry felt he was able to "stand alone."

However, things became complicated when he fell in love with a non-Christian girl. At a time in his life when marriage was becoming more important to him, Larry felt caught between his Christian faith and his love for Ann. He felt an urgency to communicate his faith to Ann hoping that she would become a Christian. Since he was on the verge of completing his degree, thoughts of career and family life were becoming more prominent. Larry was feeling increased tension between the need for personal intimacy and marriage and the desire to remain faithful to his Christian beliefs. He was prepared to forfeit the relationship with Ann if Christ would not be at the center of their life together. Yet he also felt the pain of that decision.

In examining the development of faith in this transition period, a total of eleven individuals were interviewed (four women, seven men). The relationship between school, career, and the will of God was the predominate theme that emerged during the interviews. The women tended to be just as concerned about their careers as did the men. Marriage, on the whole, did not surface as a primary concern for most of the men and women who were interviewed, although it was still present as a developmental issue.

As we examine the development of faith during this early adult transition period, we see that it is directly tied to the separation from one's family and related developmental tasks associated with this phase of the life cycle. The primary focus of faith was frequently upon content. The main question was, "What do I believe and why?" At the same time, faith in God became less associated with some creed and became more of a personal relationship.

"Go," said Jesus, "your faith has healed you." (Mark 10:52).

7
The Late Twenties
and Early Thirties

The transition into the adult world can be a turbulent experience. The separation from family and friends combined with the pressure to firm up choices concerning career, marriage, and overall life direction can make this a trying time. Initial choices are often in place by the mid-twenties, but there is an underlying sense that some, if not the majority of those choices are provisional. Marriage and a full-time job may contribute to greater stability, but by the late twenties new feelings of restlessness may begin to emerge. In part, this is because the individual now has several years of experience which provide preliminary data to evaluate earlier choices. A sense may also develop that if certain choices are not made now, they may become increasingly difficult to make in the future.

For the Christian during this period, faith development closely parallels the significant developmental tasks related to family and career. The intellectual concerns that were important earlier centering around What do I believe? begin to give way to practical issues of Christian life and responsibility. In this chapter we will examine the lives of five individuals as they prepared for and made their way into the decade of the thirties.

Brian Dunn, Age Twenty-eight

Brian Dunn's life clearly portrayed the transition from intellectual concerns to the practical expression of faith. Prior to age fourteen, Brian's basic faith in the validity of Christianity was never in doubt. Once in high school, though, he began to experience problems.

"I had a lot of frustration with my social life because of my conservative Christian family. I felt there was a stigma because I couldn't dance and had to go to church on Sunday nights. I was embarrassed by the 'religiousness' of my family. We were going to church all the time and always prayed out loud at restaurants.

"My mother did not want us to have non-Christian friends. I always felt strange about that. As I got older my faith became very cerebral. Christianity became more of a philosophy than a way of life. I did not enjoy my little Christian subculture. I didn't like to connect my faith with my lifestyle. I didn't rebel, but I didn't accept my little Christian subculture either.

"All through high school I felt like I was going through life as an observer. I really wanted to get away from home."

Leaving home though did not solve Brian's problems. His struggle with faith continued to be an important issue.

"In my freshman year at Wheaton college I wrestled with my faith— do I want to believe this at all? Wheaton also had rules about dancing and drinking. The college replaced my parents.

"My girl friend stayed in Milwaukee. She was still in high school when I went to Wheaton. My parents were somewhat suspect of her because her parents didn't go to church.

"She was not part of our subculture. I always felt like I was never part of the real world. I couldn't develop a good relationship with her because of my lifestyle.

"When she dumped me it caused me to decide between the 'real world' and my Christian subculture. It made me more committed to my faith. I wanted more of a relationship with Christ and not a Christian subculture that moralized everything.

"My mother put everything in a moral context: hair, dress, dances—the whole bit. Everything was black and white, right or wrong. Guilt was associated with everything. The lack of freedom is what I rebelled against. She put a significance on things that I would rather find out for myself. I wanted a more free environment where everything wasn't dictated."

Later, Brian began to feel that his intellectual concerns had to be put into a more balanced perspective. Other issues were beginning to surface in his life.

"I began to realize that this intellectualizing process was not Christian either. I had to live, not just observe.

"My leaving Wheaton gave me an opportunity to live in the 'real world.' I never had the freedom to let Christianity flow out.

"Since then I have had the opportunity to see how my faith affects living my life without someone telling me what it should be. I was finding me. There wasn't an outside system like Wheaton or my parents telling me what to do.

"Since then I've gotten married and we have two children. The transition to the 'real world' was not traumatic. I feel comfortable among non-Christians. I can be honest with them and feel like I'm being myself.

"My faith has become less intellectual, and more a part of my everyday life. I now see my job, family, and friends as a response to God. The last six months I feel more directed to let my life be worship of God. Faith is now more related to everything I do."

Brian arrived at a new point of maturity in the expression of his faith. Faith had stopped becoming an object for intellectual inspection and had started to become a central dimension to the structure of his life. Faith directed him to let his life be "worship of God." Earlier, faith had been reduced to a moralistic code. Later it became an intellectual expression. Finally, it was becoming the fabric of his life.

The Apostle Paul taught that our spiritual worship was to present ourselves to God as living sacrifices, holy and pleasing to him (Rom. 12:1). For our faith to mature, it must stop becoming an object that we discuss to become an expression of who we are in Christ. It must move from being external to being internal. This process can create its own struggles as is illustrated in the life of Roberta Spire.

Roberta Spire, Age Twenty-seven

Roberta Spire once thought that she had her life figured out, but then she was no longer sure. Married with no children, Roberta worked part-time and attended college part-time.

Roberta described her childhood as being an unhappy time. Her parents fought a lot, which left her with many unpleasant memories. Her earliest concept of God came from a children's book she remembered reading when she was four years old. One image that had been important to her was an angel that cared for children. That book helped her to believe that "God was nice even when other people were not." That was especially important to her while she was growing up because she felt that her own father had been cruel to her. Later it became difficult for Roberta to feel God's love because of the image she had developed of her own father.

When Roberta was about eleven or twelve, a lady told her that God was coming back to earth and that the world would come to an end. That increased the tension that she had already been experiencing at home. Roberta continued going to the Methodist church through high school even though her parents did not attend.

After Roberta graduated from high school she attended college. During that time she became less concerned about God. She also felt unsocialized and found it difficult to relate to people. After two years Roberta dropped out of college and returned to Chicago where she got a job. Three years later she married Steve, who was a Christian that she had met at church.

Soon after that, Roberta decided to finish her degree and enrolled in a nearby Christian college. It was at that point that she began to ask serious questions about her faith.

"When I started taking courses I realized I didn't have everything worked out. I had always thought that as I got older that God's will would become more clear. That's how I felt when I was in junior high and high school.

"But now I realize that I don't have all the answers and I don't really know what will happen—whether it will be good or evil, but I've got to go on believing in God anyway."

Roberta found herself in an intensive search trying to understand where her life was headed. Once she thought she had answered that question. Later she found herself in the midst of a major reorientation.

"The most important task I'm facing is to restructure my inner self both mentally and spiritually. This includes all aspects of my personality. I have to define what it means to believe in God and identify the actions that should follow. I simply can't define my lifestyle without doing these things.

"I think a lot of people have things figured out by now. I don't know if I ever will. I use to think it was buying a home, but what is it that God wants?"

Roberta had an intellectual experience of faith but desired more than that.

"My father's influence has made it hard to experience God's love. I know that God loves me, but I would like to feel God's love more. I have a longing to become more complete in him. I know that something is missing in my life. I feel like I'm dealing with issues that most people don't face until they're forty."

While Roberta did not feel that she was experiencing a crisis, she did feel extremely unsettled. Transition periods, like the one from the late twenties to the early thirties, are characterized by these kind of feelings. Roberta had begun to review and reevaluate earlier life choices and values. She felt a sense of disparity in her life between where she was and where she wanted to be. She sensed the need to restructure her inner self. Feelings of uncertainty led her to question what God's will was for her life, an issue she believed she had settled earlier but which had resurfaced.

Roberta was concerned about the practical implications of her faith. She was beginning to feel that perhaps some of her questions would never be answered. Nevertheless, she had resolved "to go on believing in God anyway." The issue of trust becomes a key developmental concern related to the expression of faith during this period. This is further illustrated in the life of Robert Warner.

Robert Warner, Age Twenty-nine

Robert Warner became a Christian when he was in high school. One of his teachers invited him to a Young Life group. After attending several meetings, Bob began to feel that something was missing in his life—a personal relationship with Christ. Later, his commitment to Christ made a profound influence on his life.

"When I became a Christian I was real enthusiastic. I went to college and became real involved in campus ministry. One of the leaders was a guy I really admired. I saw him as a person God was really using.

"During my junior year our leader got cancer and began to suffer real bad. I didn't understand why God didn't heal him. I used to visit him at home, but after awhile I couldn't be around him anymore because it hurt too bad."

After that event, Bob's earlier enthusiasm began to give way to serious reflection concerning his Christian faith.

''The cancer caused me to question and ask why things like that happen. I expected God to give me a rational answer or I couldn't accept it. In terms of my faith, it made me realize that there are going to be some open-ended questions in life. Since then my faith has become less enthusiastic. It was like the end of my childhood faith. But I've matured. When I had a low five years ago I would question God. Now I know he's there. I used to always be looking for role models. Now I see myself as a role model. People are looking to me and my wife for stability.''

Bob sensed that people were now looking to him for answers. Faith, though, could no longer simply be expressed dogmatically. Nor could it be based upon emotions; rather, faith had to become an expression of trust in God regardless of circumstances or feelings. While Christians frequently hear that message proclaimed from the pulpit, it is not until one is tested that such trust becomes a living personal reality.

Bob was beginning to feel that he was a role model for others. People were looking to him for stability, but at the same time, Bob was struggling with his own personal concerns. He had questions about his own career and wondered if he was doing what he wanted to do for the rest of his life.

Issues related to career are very prominent during early adulthood. During the early twenties there is pressure to decide on a career direction. By the late twenties, if a vocation has not been selected, the pressure to choose one begins to intensively mount. By that time, most individuals have been working in some occupation for several years.

During the late twenties it is not uncommon to make an evaluation concerning career choice and to review what one has done up to that time. This review may lead to feelings of satisfaction for some or a cause of concern for others. The late twenties and early thirties are a time when many individuals commonly make modifications concerning career direction. For Ralph Banks, the change in careers was an expression of a maturing trust in God.

Ralph Banks, Age Thirty

A high school teacher, Ralph Banks was married and had two children. Ralph grew up in the Catholic church. His earlier memories of church, however, were not very pleasant. When he would attend Mass as a child, he would leave feeling guilty and depressed. He would go to confession but it did not relieve his feelings of guilt. Ralph began to doubt if there was a God. He continued attending church through high school because of his parents. Yet at the same time, he detested it.

Once Ralph left home to go to college, he left the church. His attention turned to sports, particularly wrestling where he was a member of the college team. In Ralph's words, "I finally felt free. I was going to party. My carnal man was alive and well and I wasn't going to waste the new opportunity I had."

However, things did not develop as Ralph had hoped. As a sophomore he was bumped from the wrestling team by two incoming freshmen. Ralph felt like his world was collapsing.

"I was searching and decided to pledge a fraternity. Several of the brothers were Christians and they invited me to a prayer meeting. I knew they had something I needed. It was in this group that I found the Lord. For the first time since being a little boy I felt clean inside. It took away years of guilt and assured me that God loved me. At that time I wasn't sure if anyone loved me."

After Ralph graduated from college, he got married and was hired as a high school physical education teacher. His wife Sandy, who was also a Christian, received a job as a teacher too. Things could not have been going better for either of them.

After several years they bought a new home and made the decision to start a family. Sandy stopped working to care for the baby after it was born. At first finances were tight, but Ralph completed his master's degree and received a raise. It was at that time that Ralph began to raise new questions concerning his future.

"A major event occurred in 1979 when I began to feel the call of God to become a minister. I was ready to go to seminary but then I felt God say no. I checked out a seminary but I knew it was the wrong thing to do. I had a good job with a good income, I felt the call to the ministry was a mistake.

"Shortly after that, I felt the call again. Work became difficult. I prayed in desperation and a sense to preach the gospel came over my life. Sandy and I decided that I would teach one more year and then go to school and become a minister."

It was during that time that a major change occurred in Ralph's expression of faith and his relationship to God.

"When I was in college I had faith to believe God for whatever he told me to do. I had faith for a job and I got it. Everything was fulfilled.

"I began to express faith at work that God would promote me. I was highly motivated to coach and teach. My faith had a lot of carnality such as trying to get ahead in my profession. I wanted to have winning teams and to have the administration feel good about me as a teacher. Even though I prayed and read the Bible everyday, I didn't really lean on Christ.

"Then things became difficult at work. I felt like a complete failure. At first I became depressed. I prayed for three days and felt sorry for myself. I tried to please God.

"Then I began to read the Book of Psalms. The Lord came into my life like streams of living water. He removed all my fear and gave me assurance that success in the world's eyes was not success in his eyes. My life had not been a failure! Now I realize that I can't do it on my own. I've learned not to lean on the flesh."

Ralph's review of his life and the decision to stop teaching to become a minister came during the transition period from the twenties to the thirties. Prior to that time, faith had been somewhat of a mechanical process—tell God what you want and he will do it for you. Furthermore, this understanding of faith had seemed to work for Ralph. He had prayed for his job and had received it. He asked for a promotion and it came. But then things began to turn bad. His coaching career was not what he had hoped for. Ralph felt unsettled in his spirit. He was no longer sure that he wanted to be a teacher the rest of his life. He felt uncertain about his future. He thought God was leading him into the ministry, but he was not sure.

Beginning at about age twenty-seven, Ralph began to experience a major transition in his life. Over a two-year period he struggled with his career. Feeling both the leading of God and frustration at work, Ralph made the decision to enter the ministry. Since this interview was completed, Ralph has left teaching to become the pastor of a new congregation. He is moving into his thirties having made a significant change in both career and income.

Ralph's faith has also changed. Faith is no longer taken for granted. In his twenties Ralph saw faith as one way to legitimize his own career goals. He really did not depend on God; instead, he pursued his goals on his own strength and when they did not work out he felt like a failure.

It was then, through reading the Bible, that Ralph realized that he was not a failure. There was a new recognition that God measured success differently than Ralph. Through that experience, Ralph discovered a new freedom to trust his life and career with God.

When Ralph left home to attend college he was not a Christian. While that was a time to explore his own values and lead his own life, he really did not experience an intellectual struggle concerning faith. God was unimportant to Ralph until his world started to cave-in. Ralph's faith was prompted by his own identity struggle and the need to be accepted, to be loved. Christian friends helped Ralph to encounter God in a life changing way. Once faith became real to him, the main issues that emerged were not intellectual, but centered around occupational progress. Yet faith remained self-centered. He prayed for a job and sought to be promoted.

While Ralph's faith had an emotional impact on his life, it simply became an extension of his own goals and personal aspirations. During his late twenties, when he began to experience frustration with his career and had doubts concerning his future, his faith reached a point of spiritual crisis. Ralph realized that his faith in God had been self-serving. It was only when things took a turn for the worse that he recognized the need to yield his life more completely to the Lord. At that point, faith took on a new dimension of trust.

My interviews indicated that both men and women in early adulthood maintained concerns related to career. During the early twenties these concerns differed very little between the sexes. However, once marriage occurred and children arrived, the demands of motherhood had a far greater impact on the career concerns of women than did fatherhood on men. Nevertheless, both men and women experienced related concerns pertaining to faith development. These concerns are illustrated in the life of Judy Potter.

Judy Potter, Age Thirty-two

The mother of two small girls, Judy Potter spent most of her time as a housewife. Her husband Frank was a minister. Looking back over her life, Judy was able to see how earlier decisions in her life had fit together like pieces of a jigsaw puzzle.

When Judy was three years old her mother died. Her father remarried two years later, but Judy never felt close to her stepmother. Her grandmother became a very important person in her life and took Judy to church. During vacation Bible school, at the age of eight, Judy accepted Christ as her Savior. She felt a new sense of security. However, things did not go well at home and at age thirteen she experienced severe emotional trauma. Judy had feelings of depression and harbored deep resentment toward her stepmother. She met with a child psychologist for over one year.

After she graduated from high school and left home, Judy felt more confident about her life. She attended college and after that seminary. Her feelings of self-worth increased as she left home and made some choices on her own which she felt good about.

After seminary Judy got married and started working at a church. Shortly thereafter, at age twenty-six, she began to experience emotional trauma again with intense feelings of anger toward her stepmother. Finally, she was hospitalized and underwent counseling which helped her a great deal.

A year later she and Frank moved to the West Coast where Frank became pastor of a small congregation. Judy became pregnant and at age thirty gave birth to their first daughter Marie. However, she found it very difficult to love her new baby. Unexpectedly, she became pregnant again. Sensing the need for emotional support, she began attending Parents Anonymous, an organization to help parents. A year after the birth of her second daughter, she felt like the major emotional difficulties were behind her. Throughout the past ten years, Judy had seen a major change in the expression of her faith.

"Since the children have come my faith has changed. Earlier in my life I didn't feel the need for faith as much. It was more of an intellectual experience, something that was interesting to discuss. Now I know the Shepherd and not just the psalm. The personal relationship that I have with God is important. The Bible has become a source of comfort to me. Before it was just a book of facts.

"I've also been thinking more about my own sense of self-worth. Since the children have come I ask myself, How will I leave my mark on the world? Now I see that guiding young people is important. I enjoy the children and am now working at the church with the children."

At that same time, Judy was also facing other important issues.

"I've been thinking more about my parents. They're getting wrinkled and gray. I realize that they are aging and so am I. I feel that I'm at a crossroads. Just as I needed them, they will also need me.

"I'm also trying to balance my time as a mother with that of a wife and also find time for myself. I think more about things like money and buying a house or car. I've also thought about going back to work."

In looking back over her life, Judy had seen God become more of a personal reality for her. God had become a shepherd, not simply an intellectual abstraction. He had helped her to cope with intense emotional conflict. Judy felt less rigid and more tolerant toward others. Earlier in her life she had just seen one way of doing things, but later she had become open to new ideas. She had also been able to develop a new attitude toward her stepmother. In Judy's words, "The Bible speaks of forgiveness. I've been able to lay at rest some of my anger toward my stepmother."

Summary

The late twenties and early thirties are a major transitional period. For those who have not married or finalized a career direction, the pressure begins to increase to do so. One's internal sense of social timing indicates that it is time to act now or it may become too late.

Individuals who selected careers or who had married earlier, find this a time to evaluate former decisions and begin preparation for the thirties. This may include becoming parents. If the wife has been working, parenthood will result in greater domestic responsibilities. Additional struggles may surface related to career loss, to feelings of being trapped at home, or to concerns related to childcare. Financial pressures may begin to mount. The husband may wrestle with his own vocation and wonder if he is really doing what he wants to do. He senses that while it is not too late to change career direction, it will become increasingly more difficult to do so in the future.

At least one noticeable aspect of faith development emerged during this period. It was the movement from faith as an intellectual object to faith as a personal experience of trusting in God. The demands and pressures of life have been experienced more directly. The issue is no longer, What do I believe? but What difference does my belief make?

For men this was witnessed by an increased reliance upon God rather than upon one's self. Intellectual concerns became replaced with faith responses that were more geared to the heart than to the head.

For the most part, the same was true for women. Intellectual concerns faded more into the background while trust in a personal God became more important. There was a recognition by both men and women that some questions concerning life are open-ended and may never be answered. One must decide to trust God in spite of that. That decision marks the beginning of faith from an object of belief to faith as an internal part of one's life structure.

I do not intend to imply that every Christian experiences this transition from faith as an object to faith as part of one's life. Nor am I suggesting that it occurs only at this time or only in the ways illustrated above. Yet it does appear that this is an important aspect of faith development during the age thirty transition. I would argue that this transition, however it is experienced, is critical to Christian growth and the development of mature faith. Faith is to direct one's total orientation to life. While it includes belief, that belief must become internalized and expressed through personal commitment to and trust in Jesus Christ as Lord and Savior. Issues of trust and commitment then become renegotiated throughout the rest of life. Faith development continues to be closely associated with development issues as we see in the next chapter concerning the mid-thirties.

> Therefore, since we are justified by faith, we have peace with God through our Lord Jesus Christ. (Rom. 5:1, RSV)

8
The Mid- To Late Thirties

It has been estimated that the average American family moves ten times during the first ten years of marriage. There finally comes a time when you want to throw away the boxes and stay put! The decade of the thirties is such a time. There is a growing desire to put down roots and to become established. In order for this to happen, firmer choices and commitments are required.

For men, this is a period for career advancement. As Levinson has noted, the task is to get on with the work; to begin to make one's mark in the world. By the late thirties, a number of indicators will be visible reflecting how successful one has been or will likely to be pertaining to career. For some, career success will contribute to stability as they enter middle age. For others, grave concerns will surface concerning vocation contributing to increased stress, self-doubt, anger, depression, or perhaps the desire to make a radical break with the past and to try and start over.

Career-oriented women are likely to experience similar concerns as do their male counterparts. Yet for most women, domestic responsibilities are central to their life structure during the thirties. Even if they have full-time employment, they are likely to feel that they have a full-time job at home too.

Studies have shown that marital satisfaction tends to decline after the birth of the first child. A number of factors contribute to that including major role changes for both husband and wife; concerns about health care for the infant; the mother feeling trapped at home; sleepless nights; low energy levels; decline in social activities; and increased financial responsibilities at a time when the income may have declined if the mother had given up previous employment.

This decline in marital satisfaction continues until the "empty nest" when the children have left home. The decade of the thirties, therefore, has the potential to be a time of pressure related to both career advancement and marital satisfaction. This decade can serve as a fork in the road where husbands and wives head off in different directions only to discover that they have grown apart a decade later. However, this should not be the norm for Christians. Our faith in God should make a decisive difference in how we respond to these life issues.

Christians, like all human beings, face problems. We are not immune from family difficulties or concerns related to career. Yet the power of God, working through the believer in the context of a caring community of Christians, enables us to have hope. With his help, and with the support of loving Christian friends, we can do all things through Christ! Every Christian is responsible for his or her own actions and decisions. The biblical principle is that we will reap what we sow. Therefore, as Christians we must work at building a strong and faith-oriented life structure that will sustain us as we face critical life concerns.

Several faith responses emerged as being important during the thirties. Again, these responses were closely associated with the developmental tasks related to this period, particularly with career and family life. For men, the issue of trust in God, as opposed to trusting in one's self, continued to be a prominent issue. Intellectual concerns continued to decline in importance. For women, the sustaining power of God to cope with life problems became a more important expression of faith. From the thirties on, trust in God continues to be a prominent issue throughout life. Trust must be continually renegotiated in the midst of changing circumstances. In this chapter we will examine the development and expression of faith by four men and three women in their mid- to late thirties as they wrestled with issues pertaining to career, family life, self-worth, and divorce.

Phil Carpenter, Age Thirty-five

Phil Carpenter was reared in a Christian home. At age six his mother asked him if he wanted to serve God. Together they knelt at the sofa where Phil asked Jesus into his heart.

The older Phil got, the more difficult it became for him to live a Christian life. His parents had strict rules which impacted his social life while he was in high school. During that time he felt miserable. After high school Phil attended college. There he met a group of Christian friends which strengthened his own faith in God.

At the end of Phil's freshman year he met Sally. Phil saw that as a turning point in his life. Sally's entire family was a positive influence on Phil. Two years later he and Sally were married; however, their marriage ran into immediate difficulties.

"When we got married in 1967 I was twenty and Sally was seventeen. It was difficult the first two years. It took almost four or five years before she was convinced that I loved her. Our communication with one another was bad. We would have fights and disagreements. Sally moved away from home, got married and got a job all at once. It was real hard for her to adjust."

A year or so later, Phil felt like the Lord was calling him into the ministry. He decided to drop out of college to attend a Bible school, but when he and Sally arrived at school, they could not find an apartment or job. Feeling defeated, they left. According to Phil, "It really shook us."

After returning home, Phil re-enrolled at college and they both found jobs. Further marital difficulties surfaced when they decided to have a child, but then were unable to do so. Eventually Phil and Sally adopted a baby. They hoped that things would improve but they didn't. The baby was sick and according to Phil, ". . . he was allergic to everything. He didn't sleep through the entire night for at least two-and-a-half years."

By this time, Phil and Sally had stopped going to church. Under severe emotional pressure, Sally decided to file for a divorce. She did not feel she could go on any further. She left Phil but then became ill and ended up in the hospital. At that point, both Phil and Sally began to rediscover faith in God and eventually their marriage was restored.

"It wasn't just one thing that turned it around. Our son got healthier and that helped. It was a slow climb back that took two or three years.

"Sally went through some remarkable deliverances. I had some deep hurts and doubts but God did some inner healing in my life. As I saw what God was doing in Sally's life, my own faith was built up. Now I feel the Lord's love. He has done an inner healing in both of our lives.''

Before this ''inner healing'' occurred, Phil had to admit to himself that he could not solve his own problems.

''I was very independent and didn't want any help. But during this time I needed other people. It taught me that I had to accept help. That was a real growing time for me. I admitted to myself that I couldn't do it alone.''

Phil no longer felt that his career was as important to him as it once was. While the past two years of his life had been a happy time for him, he was becoming more concerned about his son who had just turned eleven years old. ''He's becoming more rebellious,'' commented Phil.

Phil and Sally were married very early. That contributed to immediate problems. Sally was insecure and felt unloved. Phil was unsure about his career, which added to their uncertainties. They wanted a child but were unable to have one. Later, after they adopted a baby, he was sick and required constant attention. Their marriage was falling apart.

During that time both Sally and Phil became less involved in church. As their problems reached a crisis proportion, they began to seek God for help. Earlier they had depended upon themselves but were unable to adequately cope. Before true healing could occur, Phil had to admit that he needed assistance. This led to a new trust in others and especially God.

The theme of trust was prominent during the thirties throughout all of the interviews. Frequently individuals, and particularly men, would arrive at a point where they realized they needed help. There was an awareness that they could not make it on their own power. Sometimes the need was related to one's marriage or children. Other times it was related to career. These situations led to a new expression of faith as illustrated in the lives of Dwain Saunders and Samuel Gibbons.

Dwain Saunders, Age Thirty-five

The biggest influence in Dwain Saunder's Christian growth had been his wife Stacey. Without her support, he was unsure whether he would still have been a Christian.

Dwain first became a Christian when he was eighteen, while dating Stacey. Stacey came from a strong Christian family but Dwain had rarely attended church. Several years later they were married.

Dwain's primary goal in life was to make money. He invested all of his time and energy into building a successful construction business. In a short time, his faith in God had become replaced with faith in himself. Church was no longer important. In his early thirties Dwain experienced a major financial setback. He faced a situation beyond his control.

"When I first became a Christian, I had a measure of faith. But I went off on my own and my faith changed from trusting in the Lord to trusting in myself. I became consumed with my career and making money. We owned an apartment building and someone torched it. It was a total loss. I experienced tremendous fear—to the point that I was afraid for my own life. I didn't know if anyone had died in the fire or not. I was totally afraid.

"One thing after another began to go bad. We started having financial problems because of the economy. My whole construction business was going under."

By age thirty-five Dwain had experienced total financial failure. That experience caused him to reassess his goals in life and his relationship with God.

"I realized I needed more faith. I've come full swing from being materialistic to now having spiritual goals. I used to want to be a millionaire. Now I don't care about that anymore. I just want to be able to pay my bills. My life isn't centered around money any more. Today we're bankrupt and my faith has never been greater."

The drive to "make it" is a powerful force during the thirties and the forties. It is one that can easily become self-consuming. For men their own feelings of self-worth are frequently tied to their career. Success, or the lack of it, can affect these feelings. Jesus said, "What good is it for a man to gain the whole world, yet forfeit his soul?" (Mark 8:36). Nevertheless, social pressures to succeed, to make it, to be somebody can grip the heart of a man in his thirties. Jesus' proclamation, "But seek first his kingdom and his righteousness . . . " (Matt. 6:33) comes into direct conflict with the marketplace. Faith in God can easily become replaced with faith in one's self if the goal of "making it" becomes the primary focus of one's life. A person can go to church, tithe, and manifest outward signs of faith, yet still be consumed with self-interests. When this is done, there is no escaping worry, anxiety, or frustration. Without trust there can be no peace; the Christian must compete against an unknown future just like the non-Christian. This was the experience of Samuel Gibbons until he met Christ as Savior during his mid-thirties.

Samuel Gibbons, Age Thirty-nine

Samuel Gibbons never knew his father. He grew up on his grandparents' farm in Iowa. Although his grandparents took him to church, it had minimal influence on him. Once Samuel left home, God had little, if any, place in his life.

Samuel was married at age twenty-one and became employed as a computer technician. He and his wife did well financially and bought their first home three years later. When he was twenty-nine, he and his wife adopted a baby boy. While the new addition created quite an adjustment in their lifestyle, it was a joyful time as well. Three years later they adopted a baby girl and moved into a new, larger home. Samuel described it as a hard time, but also one of high satisfaction. However, the next four years of Samuel's life took a turn for the worse.

"It was a time in my life when I was seeking respect from other men. I had come up the hard way and wanted to prove myself. We had purchased some investment property and suddenly I was running into walls. It seemed like everything I touched turned sour. I started calling out to God, 'What are you doing to me?' I was always getting knocked off the ladder and would have to climb back up. At the same time my wife got a job as a secretary and was becoming more independent of me."

During that time, Samuel's wife began to attend church. She prayed that Samuel would come with her. Finally he did.

"I decided one Sunday morning to go to church. I was raised in a Christian home, but rebelled after I was married. I didn't go to church until I was thirty-six. My wife started going and she would cry and wanted me to take her and the kids to church. We went that Sunday and they had communion. The minister gave an altar call and I got so convicted that I couldn't breathe normally. I was nervous. The same spirit hit my wife and we both ran to the altar."

During the following three years, Samuel developed a new perspective on his life and faith.

"Now life is worth living. I know now that I don't have to please man, only God. We're becoming a family again and are trying to raise our children in a Christian home.

"Earlier my goals were to be something. Now I want to grow in Christ.

He has given me gifts and I want to be responsible. My goals aren't with my job anymore. My mind isn't upon the world. Now I want to work for the Lord. When I first believed I wasn't involved in the church. But now we're involved. Now we work with people. We're praying that our children will become Christians."

Samuel's Christian faith gave him a new perspective on success. Success became redefined in terms of his relationship to Christ. His main concern now was for his children to become Christians.

During their thirties Phil, Dwain, and Samuel all moved from being independent to recognizing the need to accept help from others. Problems related to family, career, or finances led them to a new dependency upon God. At the same time, the goal of "making it" became redefined in light of trust in God. Success took on a new meaning. Also, as their children got older, they became increasingly concerned about their children's relationship with Christ. From the hard lessons of life these men began to realize that the significance of life was not found in the abundance of one's possessions.

Unlike the men above, David Spencer had never been consumed by career or finances. In fact, he had never clearly established any goals pertaining to career. During the twenties, the lack of career goals may not cause any great problems. That is a period to explore and test out various options. But by the mid-thirties, if a career has not been clearly defined it can be a source of anxiety or conflict. It can also have an impact on the expression of faith.

David Spencer, Age Thirty-four

Until David Spencer became a Christian at age twenty-two, he felt like a social outcast. His father, who was a truck driver, was gone a lot while David was growing up. His family moved when he was thirteen and that was a traumatic time.

"I wanted to run away. I was pretty insecure and didn't want to leave my friends. It took awhile to make new friends and be accepted in high school. Since I never really was accepted I felt out of place. I was fat and never went out on dates. I didn't feel like girls accepted me."

After high school David went to college only because his dad wanted him out. Things went from bad to worse.

"I didn't have any goals and I never went to class. After the spring quarter I left and came home. I felt depressed. This was during the

Vietnam war and I tried to join the army. I had a death wish. But they wouldn't take me. I was color-blind, flat-footed and overweight.''

During the next four years David continued to live at home while he worked as an unskilled laborer. It was during that time that he experienced a major change in his life.

''My best friend finished college and came back to town. I was over at his apartment and there was this girl there who was a Christian. She started talking to us about the Lord and invited us to church. I could see that she was honest so I thought I would give it a shot. I had just broken up with a girl at that time.

''I usually went out drinking on Sunday nights but I went to church with her and got saved. I was out of work at the time and spent the next month reading the Bible.''

Later David was hired at a Christian bookstore where he had access to books that helped him to grow as a Christian. In 1973 he got married at the age of twenty-five and a year later their first child was born. During the next four years he changed jobs and moved several times. It was a difficult period for his wife who felt lonely and without many friends.

In 1978 David settled into a more permanent job as a custodian and maintenance man for the school district. Although David was very active in his local church, he found himself struggling with his own Christian life and career. He had seen major changes in his life since he had become a Christian and was thinking more about his future.

''Right now I'm trying to decide whether I'm going to remain in my present vocation. It's somewhat threatening to think about it. I wonder whether I'm stagnated as a Christian. I feel like I've reached a plateau. I seem to be doing the same thing over and over again. I've felt this way for six months.''

Both the routine of his work and involvement in church had led David to feel stagnated. He wanted to move beyond where he was, but was unsure of how to go about doing it. At the same time, David was placing an increasing importance upon his family. He wanted God to be at the center of his home.

''The most important task I'm facing now is raising my children in the Lord. While I was growing up my mother did almost everything for me. The biggest change I need to make is to be less selfish and more responsible as a husband and a man. My only goal in life is to remain faithful to God and to see that my family does too.''

David also felt less rigid than he did when he first became a Christian.

"In my early years I tried to gain Bible knowledge and was proud of that. Now I've become more centered on showing love and consideration for people. I'm more tolerant of those who believe differently from me. What's important now is to be an example."

David found God in the midst of a transition period in his life. He had found little social acceptance, had broken up with a girl, and was trying to establish himself as an adult. At first his faith was concerned with "knowing" about God. He studied the Bible and was proud of his knowledge. After he was married, the important issues became those which affected people. As David entered the thirties, he became less rigid and more tolerant of those who were different from him. His attention turned more toward his family and his responsibilities as a husband. At age thirty-four he still wondered about his career but had no clear goals. His main concern was to be a "faithful" man. Feeling somewhat stagnated, he desired to grow closer to God, but was unsure of what the next step in his life should be.

Not everyone experiences financial problems or major concerns related to career, though for many, trust in God becomes an important expression of faith during the thirties. There is much less concern about dogma, doctrine, or ritual and more concern about coping, persevering and growing as a person. The longer a person lives, the more likely they will experience some situation over which they have no control. During that time when they need help, encouragement, or comfort, the Christian may express a new dimension of trust in God. Such trust may be expressed in numerous ways. For some it means that God will provide for a need. It may be a healing, a job, the resolution of a conflict, or a financial concern. For others it may mean that God will sustain them as they face a crisis or given them power to endure a difficult situation. However it appears, trust in God plays a central role in the expression of faith, particularly from the late twenties on.

During the twenties, the issue of God's will becomes important as the young adult attempts to sort out his or her future. Once major choices have been made, God's will tends to be taken for granted. However, directional questions tend to resurface throughout life, especially during transitional periods. Major transitions often prompt individuals to seek God for direction. This became an important issue for Linda McDonald after she was divorced. It required a new dimension of trust.

Linda McDonald, Age Thirty-five

Linda McDonald was raised in a Baptist church. She felt that God was the most important person in her life until she was sixteen or seventeen. She then went through a fifteen-year period which did not include God at all.

While growing up, Linda's most meaningful relationships occurred within her family and church. She faithfully studied the Bible and during her teen-aged years began to feel that God was calling her to be a missionary. When she was fourteen she began to struggle with what she perceived to be a sense of apathy in the church.

"It seemed like people didn't take things seriously enough. I started to become critical. I was gung-ho and it seemed like my teachers at church were unprepared. I was bored to death and didn't want to go to Sunday School anymore. After that I became argumentative and tension developed between me and my parents. Other kids were dropping out of church and they seem uncommitted."

During senior high, Linda became painfully aware that there were no Christian boys to date at the church. She began to feel pressure to date non-Christians. Eventually this led to a non-Christian marriage followed by marital problems.

"The first person that I began to seriously date later became my husband. He was very intelligent. He was able to relate to me, but fanned my cynicism about the church into flame. He had a very strong influence on me.

"While I still went to church, I started to develop new ideas about it. He was the first person I dated and my parents didn't like him. That just added to the tension."

After graduating from high school, Linda went to college just to get away from home. She was attending a Christian college, but confused she dropped out after one year and decided to attend the same university as her boyfriend. After her junior year in 1968 they were married. By that time church was no longer a part of her life. Ten years later they were divorced.

After the divorce, at age thirty-one, Linda realized that her life was out of her control. A secretary in her office, who was a Christian, began to share her faith with her. One week later, Linda started attending church again for the first time in ten years. During the next four years Linda spent a great deal of time reflecting about her past and her future.

"I am convinced that before I was fourteen I was in God's will. The ten-year period after that I was completely alien to God. Before I wanted to be a missionary. Now I ask, 'God, can you still do that with me?'

"I didn't do what he wanted me to do. I moved out of the path. Now I wonder if God will bring me back to fulfill his will. I don't have the same, 'I know, I know' as I did as a kid. I'm not sure if I should rest in the Lord or if I should go out there and find out what I should be."

Linda was experiencing a struggle with her future.

"I'm very impatient waiting for God to act. Yet I feel I have so much to grow in my relationship with him. My desire is to be involved in ministry. I never found being divorced a problem until I started writing to mission boards. Apparently, they have no need for the divorced. It makes me sorrowful because now I realize that my past has closed a lot of doors."

Linda was looking to God for direction in her life. She no longer thought it would be as cut and dried as it was when she was a child. Yet she did expect to discover an assurance and a sense of peace concerning God's direction for her. Even though she felt she may not know all the answers, God would still be with her. For her, that was the important thing to know.

The expression of faith is affected by many factors including finances, family life and career. A person's self-image and self-esteem also affect the development and manifestation of faith. This was especially true for Vicki Bloom.

Vicki Bloom, Age Thirty-six

Vicki Bloom struggled with unresolved childhood memories. She bore a deep emotional scar from not feeling loved as a child. Vicki grew up in San Francisco. Her father worked in a restaurant from 7:00 A.M. until 10:00 P.M. six days a week. Vicki felt totally rejected by her mother. On her father's day off, he would spend time with the children, but that stopped when her parents were divorced when Vicki was eleven. Not only did she feel unloved at home, but Vicki also felt rejected at school. These feelings affected her relationship with God. She felt that love was conditional, even from God.

"If I did the right things God would love me. I didn't feel that his love was a free gift. I always had to justify myself. I couldn't be loved just because I was Vicki."

Once Vicki left home she felt less pressure. During her mid-twenties, she met Jeff and sensed that everything would change for the better. At first they were drawn together by common bonds of spiritual concern. After a meaningful courtship period they were married. Soon, though, Vicki felt neglected by Jeff. She thought he was too busy with his work and again she felt unloved. Her faith in God began to slip away.

"I stopped reading the Bible and praying. When I would talk to Jeff about the scriptures, he would say that I wasn't interpreting them right. I began to feel further away from God. I felt like God didn't love me. I thought, I'm so horrible, how could he love me? I felt guilty."

Vicki finally reached a point of despair.

"I just gave up. I became so miserable that I didn't want to grow as a person or a Christian. I came to a place where everything was destroyed. I don't know how I made it. I must have had a little hope. Somehow I knew that Christ was there."

Slowly, Vicki began to see her life change for the better.

"I knelt down one day. I knew I couldn't depend on anyone. I said, 'Well God, it's me and you.' I had to admit that I had some responsibility for myself—either to become happy or to stay miserable. Little by little I started reading some books. They really helped me. I once again have hope. I'm starting to reach out to others. What I've gone through has made me more compassionate.

"I feel I am growing now. I can't say that I'm happy, but I realize that God loves me and accepts me for who I am."

Vicki still struggled with feelings of low self-esteem as well as with her marriage. She felt she had to lower her expectations in order to have hope for a happier life. Through her own experiences as a mother, God was teaching her about unconditional love. She recognized that her faith had changed.

"I have a new sense of perseverance. I'm starting to realize some of my inner qualities. Sometimes I still undergo false guilt, but I realize that God loves me. If anything defeats me, it's that I don't have any goals. I want to encourage people because I know what it's like to be discouraged."

Vicki had struggled with feelings of self-esteem and self-worth for most of her life. As a child she only felt loved when she pleased people. Later those feelings were transferred to God. She felt that God's love was conditional too.

At first she thought her marriage was the long-awaited answer.

However, as her husband became more involved in his career she became increasingly depressed. She finally reached a point where there was no one left but God.

Looking to God for help, Vicki realized that she had to take responsibility for her own actions. As she prayed, read books, and began to reach out to others she discovered new hope. She realized that God accepted her unconditionally. That helped Vicki to accept herself.

While things did not change all at once, Vicki had developed a new sense of perseverance. She recognized that God could use her to help others. While she endeavored to identify personal goals, she now knew that she had inner qualities that were important.

In the final example in this chapter we will encounter a woman whose faith enabled her to endure a difficult life situation. Without faith, she was unsure what she would have done.

Mary Bradshaw, Age Thirty-four

Mary Bradshaw grew up in Mississippi where her father worked in a lumber mill. She was married at the age of fifteen. Shortly after that, she and her husband moved to Kentucky where he worked as a coal miner. Several years and several children later, Mary found her life to be miserable and depressing. One Sunday she and her children went to church. There Mary gave her heart to Christ.

"I became a Christian but it only lasted for three months. Life was difficult for us. I didn't go to church for several years. Finally, my two little girls went to stay with my mom. I went to stay with her too. My husband lost his job and we all started going to church again. I got saved, then a couple months later my husband got saved too."

Over the past ten years, Mary's family life has continued to deteriorate.

"My husband didn't stay a Christian long. He stopped going to church and it wasn't long before my faith went downhill because of family problems. I read this gospel tract and it scared me and blessed me. I knew that I wanted to be a Christian."

Faith in Christ helped Mary to cope with family problems. Yet things were not easy. In order to find employment, her husband had to work out of town and was home only on the weekends. This created additional financial burdens. Mary's daughters were now teen-agers and were struggling with their own identity crises.

"My kids occupy my time now. My husband has to work away from home and he's only here on the weekends. Of course he needs money to live where he is and we need it here. My daughters are teen-agers and are more rebellious now. This time in my life is very difficult. I think a lot about my husband and my daughters.''

Mary's faith did not extend much beyond her own immediate needs. She was so consumed by just trying to survive that she had little emotional energy left to invest elsewhere. Her being married at an early age and her becoming a teen-aged mother restricted her options throughout early adulthood. For Mary, faith in God helped her to endure. She had hope both for her family and her future even though her situation was oppressive.

Summary

Interview findings indicated that the development and expression of faith during the mid-thirties was affected by developmental issues related to both career and family life. Trust in God tended to increase when problems surfaced or there was a lack of personal direction.

For the men, financial and career concerns prompted a new relationship with God. One theme that emerged on several occasions was an awareness for the need of outside help. There were feelings of ''we can't make it on our own strength.'' This recognition led to increased trust in God as well as in others. When this took place, it was often accompanied by a reassessment of career and family goals. Success became redefined in terms of one's relationship with Christ rather than in terms of finances or career. There also tended to be a heightened concern for family life, especially for children as they approached the teen-aged years.

In our one example of divorce, it prompted a new concern for life direction and seeking God's will. This was true with similar cases as well. Earlier choices and commitments had to be reassessed in the light of changing circumstances. For Linda McDonald, this brought the painful realization that her divorce had closed certain doors for Christian service. While she sought direction, she no longer expected simple answers like she would have earlier in life. Yet she did expect to have a sense of peace concerning the decisions she ultimately would make.

By the mid-thirties, a person's life is more firmly structured in a network of relationships, commitments, and responsibilities. This is particularly true if a person is married and has children. Circumstances and issues that affect one person can have a rippling effect into the lives of others. For example, the decision of a married man to change careers or file for a divorce affects many other people, but none more than his own family members.

It is a myth that one can make a clean break with the past. The longer we live, the more our lives become embedded in a structure that becomes increasingly difficult to change. That is not to say that conversion does not give us a new beginning. It does. No matter what situation we find ourselves in, Jesus Christ can bring new life. This new life does not alter our environment or circumstances; rather, it transforms our lives. We must then take responsibility to change our world.

By the mid-thirties, a person is reaping—for better or for worse—the results of decisions made earlier in life. The development and expression of faith is affected by those decisions. Mary Bradshaw's life was shaped by an early marriage. Once those decisions are made, they have long-term consequences.

Yet we have also witnessed how faith affects the way individuals respond to life. Faith in God helped Phil Carpenter and his wife restore a failing marriage. It enabled Dwain Saunders and Samuel Gibbons to reorient life goals and to gain a new perspective on and appreciation for life. Linda McDonald's relationship with Christ helped her to find new meaning to life following her divorce. Similar stories could be told over and over. Faith in Jesus Christ brings life. That does not mean that life circumstances become easier for the Christian. All people must face life as it comes, for better or for worse. But Jesus said, "I am the resurrection and the life. He who believes in me will live . . . " (John 11:25).

9
The Forties

A friend of mine, a university professor, recently commented, "The students look younger every year." Of course, they really are not any younger, he is getting older. Those feelings begin to grab hold more strongly once you reach the forties.

Age forty is a barrier that many people despise to cross, because it symbolizes the transition from the generation that is "with it" to the "old fogies." People over forty are part of the establishment—the status quo. Someone who is thirty-nine can still be one of the buddies, but once over forty the buddy-image is replaced by the parent-image. Levinson calls this the sequence of the generations.

The prominent faith issues that emerged during the thirties continue into the decade of the forties. Concerns related to family and career continue to affect the expression of faith. Yet, as is true throughout life, one's faith also affects the response to these and other issues. The next two chapters will examine the expression and development of faith as it relates to the era of middle adulthood.

Middle Age

Middle age is qualitatively different from both earlier and later periods in the adult life cycle. For many, it represents the prime of life. The middle-aged adult has acquired a broad range of strategies in dealing with life. Often this results in feelings of being more in command of one's self. This can also lead to a greater sense of maturity. Yet for others, middle age represents a time of turbulence and crisis. Self-examination may lead to unhappiness, disappointment and depression. Middle age is a developmental period where one begins to take stock of one's life. The middle-aged person has lived long enough to make some conclusions—for better or for worse—concerning his or her existence. The realization that life is half-over brings a new degree of sobriety to the purpose and meaning of life. For some, this reflection leads to significant changes in their life structure. For others, it reinforces earlier decisions and paves the way for a smooth transition to the second half of life.

When Does Middle Age Occur?

It is impossible to state categorically when middle age begins or ends. No one knows for sure. Likewise, no biological changes clearly define middle age for either men or women. Women do experience menopause during this time, but its effects on behavior may differ greatly from one person to the next. The lack of recognizable age boundaries lead some writers to define middle age more in terms of social and psychological developments. When age boundaries are assigned, they normally fall somewhere between thirty-five and sixty-four years of age. It must be recognized, however, that the transition to middle age, as well as the exit from it, are much less factors of age than of other more highly important and revealing indicators. These factors also interact with the development and expression of faith.

Social and Psychological Factors in Middle Age

While there are no predictable chronological events that define the transition from early adulthood into middle adulthood, there are recognizable markers that indicate that this transition is taking or has taken place.

A number of writers believe that middle age is introduced by a crisis period. Others see it as a more gradual accumulation of life problems, role transitions, physiological changes, and events that lead a person to experience him- or herself as middle-aged. One day you awaken to the reality that your life is half over. Generally this is accompanied by some serious reflection about who we are and how we feel about who we are and what we are doing. Have we accomplished what we set out to do with our lives? If so, what follows? If not, how likely is it that earlier defined goals will ever be accomplished? Normally, these questions and associated issues are embedded in broader social and psychological developments related to health, career, and family. Before examining each of these factors, let us first review the transition of Bill and Barbara Fitzhugh and the development of their faith as they entered middle age.

Bill and Barbara Fitzhugh, Ages Forty-four and Forty-five

Even though Bill and Barbara Fitzhugh had been Christians since they were children, it was during their late thirties and early forties that Christianity assumed a profound meaning for them.

During his teen-aged years, Bill described himself as "one of the squares." The only place he really felt accepted was at church. Despite these concerns, Bill did not think of it as a traumatic time.

At age seventeen, Bill left home to attend college. It was something he was looking forward to and he made a fairly smooth transition. While at college, Bill met Barbara and they were married in 1959. They both graduated and Bill went on to medical school. They found married life to be a happy time even though they had little money. During those early years together they attended the Presbyterian church.

After Bill graduated he was drafted and spent two years in the army. His spiritual life took a turn for the worse and eventually he and Barbara began to experience marital difficulties. By age forty, their marriage was in jeopardy. According to Bill, he and his wife had drifted apart.

"Going to church became rote, something to do. It didn't mean much to me anymore. We were somewhat attached to the minister, but then he moved away. The new minister didn't attract us.

"I was aggressive in my job and striving to succeed. My wife and I got to the point where we weren't communicating with each other. Our marriage was in trouble and our relationship with God was in trouble."

Bill's wife Barbara had also reached a crisis point in her own life.

"Watching my daughter grow up and leave home was the biggest change in my life. I became a mother while Bill was away in the army. It was traumatic. I missed people and felt trapped. Ever since our daughter went to kindergarten I was trying to fill a void in my life.

"When she left for college it was very traumatic for me. I was very sad. We were both scared to death to send her to college. I started feeling like my daughter didn't need me and that my husband didn't need me. Those were very down years for me."

In trying to sort out her life, Barbara turned to astrology. She still felt that something was missing in her life. Then, while watching a Christian television program, she regained a sense of hope. Recalling her early childhood memories of God, she began to seek him and pray.

During that time Barbara consulted a minister to help. She started to attend church and both she and Bill made a new commitment to Christ. Through that experience Bill developed a new outlook on his life and his faith.

"My faith today is much more profound. Before I never knew anything about the Bible. I just wanted to squeak into heaven doing as little as possible. Now I realize that I fail. I appreciate what it means to be a Christian. I'm more open and understanding than I used to be."

Bill also sensed a new urgency concerning the use of his time.

"My father died two years ago and since then I've become more aware of my own mortality. We've also had some relatives die. I have a greater sense of urgency now. I don't have time to waste. I'm concerned about the well-being of our daughter and am praying that she will find the same relationship that we have with God."

Bill is also rethinking his future.

"I'm no longer concerned about worldly things. I believe God is going to open doors for me to change careers. I feel that it's time to give back since I've received so much. One task I face is to find out where I'm going and to become what he wants me to be."

While Bill and Barbara Fitzhugh were active in church early in their lives, their spiritual commitment began to erode away during their twenties and thirties. As Bill became more involved with work and was striving to succeed, he and his wife began to drift apart. Barbara began to feel worthless. She didn't feel needed by her husband or her daughter. She sensed that there was a void in her life. Ultimately she reached a point of spiritual crisis and sought help. Through that experience, both she and Bill made a new commitment to Christ.

Bill sensed a new urgency in his life. The death of his father made him more aware of his own mortality. Bill wondered about his future and felt that he should consider a change in careers. Such a change would be a reflection of his commitment to Christ. He wanted to give after having received so much.

Bill and Barbara reflected many of the issues commonly addressed in middle age including: the launching of children into the adult world; the empty nest; death of one's parents; awareness of one's own mortality; and, career concerns. These concerns prompted Bill and Barbara to a deeper commitment to Christ. Issues related to career, family life, and aging have a profound influence on both men and women during this period.

Career

Men tend to perceive a close relationship between the life-line and the career-line. Middle age brings with it the recognition that there is a limited amount of time left to achieve personal goals and dreams. The death of friends, relatives, and associates brings this point home. This shrinkage of time and possibilities causes some men to redefine career goals and their relationship to work.

Women are more likely to see themselves in relationship to the family career. For married women with children, middle age is characterized by the launching of adolescents into the adult world. Normally this occurs over a period of years with a gradual shift in roles for both the mother and her children. Those women who have not been employed outside the home may now find themselves seeking to update occupational skills.

Unmarried women or married women without children may reflect on the family they might have had. Yet other women may enter middle age with a growing emphasis upon career goals. This latter group is likely to experience some of the same concerns about work and career as do their male counterparts.

Health and Aging.

Aging is a process that is little understood. People age at different rates because of a variety of factors including heredity and environment. Changes in the body such as the loss of or graying of hair are associated with aging. Normally, the middle-aged person experiences a heightened awareness of bodily changes. This may include a sense of slowing down, lower energy levels, more aches and pains, and for men in particular, a fear of heart problems. The death of friends and loved ones may prompt reflection concerning one's own mortality just as it did in the life of Bill Fitzhugh. The fear of chronic disease or personal decline may lead to changes in diet and lifestyle. A greater preoccupation with health concerns is one salient feature of middle age. In general, this is also associated with increased medical expenses.

Family

Families may experience their greatest periods of stress when parents are middle-aged. On the one hand, there can be tension between parents and adolescent children, who, in their own search for identity, challenge parental values and standards. On the other hand, the husband and/or wife may be faced with elderly parents in need of specialized health care and attention. All of this may occur during a time when the man is reexamining his own career goals and the woman is undergoing her own significant role changes with respect to children, husband, and work. Mounting and accumulated problems create additional family stress. This may account for the fact that the second highest peak of divorces occurs during this period. This can have a major impact on the development and expression of faith as is seen in the following two examples.

Richard Larson, Age Forty-three

Richard Larson joined the Marines when he was nineteen in an attempt to escape from an unhappy family. That was the first time in his life that he felt equal to other men his age. Because of the pressures and unhappiness that he had experienced while growing up, Dick had always envied others.

After finishing his stint in the Marines, Dick married and adjusted to a fairly normal life. He described his early years of marriage as a happy time. Later, however, his marriage deteriorated leading to a divorce when he was forty.

That same year, Dick's mother died. He described his mother as being mentally unstable and the source of much of his grief while growing up. Her death brought both feelings of relief and guilt. He felt his dad had led a miserable life because of her and hoped that her death would now free him from that. Yet he also felt guilty for feeling somewhat glad that his mother had died.

At that time, Dick was in the midst of inner turmoil. From age thirty-nine until forty-two or forty-three, he experienced a very difficult time. During that period, Dick had his first encounter with God.

"God has become important to me during the last three or four years. In the worst turmoil of your life, you have to turn to somebody."

Two years after his divorce, Dick remarried. His new wife, Ruth, helped him to become involved in church. Dick felt that God had helped him, but there were still things about his life that caused him concern.

"My new wife is a good Christian. I'm not as good as I should be. I rely on him more than before. I'm more honest with God. I try to give my problems to him which has taken some stress off me. I've asked him for help in raising my kids and with my job. I'm trying to be more patient than I've been in the past. God only gives us so much to bear. I'm learning that time heals a lot of things. I've got a new perspective on life, but I'm not sure if it comes from God or maybe from my experience. At any rate, the events of the last three years have made me rely more on others."

Since Dick has remarried, he has encountered a new set of concerns, the main one being establishing a foundation for his new marriage.

"One task I'm facing right now is getting my children and Ruth's kids raised. Her and I need to get our own routine established. I've had one kid leave home. Her daughter is sick and has been a burden on us. We don't have a normal family life. We're still apart that way. I want to see my family raised and see that they're successful in their own way. I want Ruth and me to have a successful marriage."

While Dick felt better about his life than he had just a few years ago, he was also sensing that life passes by quickly. If he was to enjoy life, he felt he had to do it now.

"You've got to stop and smell the roses. You start off expecting so much from life. You need to see some of those things done. You need to have some friends and so on. But you don't need to be obsessed with so much. We need to learn to accept the things around us. You only go around once. If you don't slow down you'll wind up going to the grave still looking for it."

Dick had developed a new perspective and felt like he knew what he wanted out of life: to see his family mature; to enjoy more financial security; to experience a happier marriage; and, to be a better Christian. He believed that God had helped him with his problems but Dick did not feel that he was as good as a Christian as he should be. In many ways Dick's faith was still immature. Concerning faith in God, Dick commented, "You can trust something if your experience tells you it's all right to trust it. You've had returns on it before. I deal with tangible experience. For example, I've given more to God and I've been rewarded with jobs."

As a new Christian, Dick had not yet entered into a relationship of unconditional trust in God. Yet he recognized the need to rely upon God and felt that God had helped him with his problems. His life circumstances brought him to a point where he knew he could not make it on his own strength. Dick sensed he needed help from others. He was not sure, though, if it was his past experience or God that prompted this new perspective on life.

The combination of unhappy childhood memories, divorce, the death of his mother, financial problems, and rearing and launching adolescent children into the adult world characterized Dick's transition into middle adulthood. It was a turbulent experience that prompted Dick to turn to God for help. Laverne Collins also found God as she entered middle age.

Laverne Collins, Age Forty

At age thirty-nine Laverne Collins reached a point where the pressure of life became unbearable. In her own words, "I had to do something with my life. My marriage had fallen apart and I was an alcoholic." After she was divorced, Laverne's problems continued. Her four children found it difficult to adjust to being without a father. Her drinking continued to be a major source of difficulty. Finally, in desperation, she went to Alcoholics Anonymous. There she encountered God.

Laverne recalled that her mother had always attended church. She felt drawn to attend church also. Although Laverne did not know any of the congregational members, she went alone that first Sunday and immediately felt accepted. One year later she felt that her life had totally changed.

"Before I found God I didn't want to live. Now I want to live. I love people. I'm learning what love is. I don't have to depend on any one person or thing. He's restoring my mind. I'm more contented and no longer feel that I'm in a constant run trying to find something."

Laverne's chief concern was her children.

"My turmoils are basically over my children. My children have seen a change in me. There are two who are accepting it and two who don't know what to do with me. My oldest daughter is rebelling against me. Yet I realize that God will take care of it. He will do it because he promised me he would. It may not be done my way, but I pray that I'll accept his way."

Laverne felt that her faith had made a significant impact on her life and attitude.

"My faith has gotten stronger and is getting stronger every day. I believe more. I love him more. I don't give up. I keep struggling. I know he will make it okay in the end. God took a mentally, physically, and spiritually abused woman at the age of forty and changed her life in one year.''

Laverne and Richard Larson both experienced a major crisis as they entered middle age. Unlike Richard, Laverne experienced a dramatic conversion that totally altered her life. Her faith in God gave her not only a new perspective on life, but a new strength and determination to make her life count. Previously she had been ready to give up. After accepting Christ she received power to change. Laverne was committed to persevere because she had hope in the future. She had a new love for people. She believed that God would change her family. Yet she was prepared to let God do it his way rather than her way. Laverne had placed her life and trust in God.

Some writers claim that middle age is ushered in by a crisis period, particularly for men. They argue that sometime between ages thirty-five and forty-five, a crisis erupts characterized by personal struggle, disenchantment, self-doubt, inner turmoil, and an urgent concern over the amount of time one has left to live. Certainly this was true of Richard Larson. Other writers question this viewpoint. While agreeing that middle age has its unique challenges and points of decision, they claim that a crisis is neither inevitable nor normative. Indeed, it is experienced by some, but other middle-aged adults experience no crisis at all.

On the basis of current research findings, it appears that this latter viewpoint is the more accurate of the two. Not everyone experiences a mid-life crisis. Furthermore, certain individuals are more likely to experience a crisis than others. Before examining these findings, however, it will be helpful to first clarify the nature of a mid-life crisis.

The Mid-Life Crisis

As we have already seen, middle age is easier to describe than to define. Generally, a number of factors pertaining to health, family, work, and appearance combine together to bring about the awareness that life does not go on indefinitely. A new outlook begins to emerge reflecting different characteristics than those expressed during the first half of life. There is a greater emphasis on personal reflection on the meaning and purpose of life. The prospect of death becomes more of a personal reality. Individual goals and dreams must be reassessed in light of the time left to carry them out. Each individual experiences certain psychological and physiological cues that indicate that middle age has arrived. When these signals begin to appear, does it mean that a personal crisis is just around the corner? Not necessarily.

The word crisis comes from the Greek work *krinein* which means "to judge, to consider, to make a decision." Middle age certainly provides ample opportunities for important decisions concerning work, health, family life, and personal commitments and values. But to what extent are these decisions associated with a crisis?

In the modern sense of the word, a crisis is a time of extreme urgency requiring special resources and help. It is a time of decision and can be a turning point for better or worse. In the Chinese language, the word "crisis" is a combination of two characters symbolizing "danger" and "opportunity." What is it that determines whether or not a crisis brings about tragedy or paves the way for personal growth and the building of character? To a large extent, the answer lies within the individual and the type of supportive network which exists around that person.

It is true that many changes occur in mid-life that have the potential to produce a traumatic situation for either the individual or his or her family. It is important to recognize, however, that a crisis does not refer simply to an event, but rather it includes one's response to that event. A crisis is an emotional state that exists in response to a traumatic experience. Initially, a person feels off-balance. The normal equilibrium of daily life is upset. In order to cope the individual must summon forth inner resources as well as rely upon outside help and support. Because people respond to circumstances differently, what might be a crisis for one is not a crisis for another.

Who Experiences a Mid-Life Crisis?

In a major research project, Michael Farrell and Stanley Rosenberg found no evidence of a universal mid-life crisis.[1] As one might expect, there are a wide range of human responses to any given set of circumstances. What causes a state of crisis for some might cause others to thrive.

Farrell and Rosenberg found that a man's family has a profound influence on his experience at mid-life. The combined influence of role changes with respect to wife and children and the effect of issues pertaining to health and career create a complex set of forces which act back upon the man. Although it is possible for a man to feel comfortable about his career, he may at the same time struggle with earlier unresolved issues in his life regarding trust, intimacy, and self-esteem. This may result in problems at home or feelings of self-doubt outside of the job. A crisis can be prompted by a number of factors. When it does occur it will affect the development and expression of faith. This is illustrated in the life of Fred Linder.

Fred Linder, Age Forty-seven

Fred Linder faced a crisis period in his life at age forty-one. It was prompted by the birth of his last child.

"Six years ago we had a little boy. He was born with Down's syndrome—a mongoloid baby. When he was born the doctor said to me, "You're a minister. Maybe it would be better if you told your wife."

At first Fred did not feel that his faith was affected. If anything, he felt it had become stronger. But the people at church began to ask questions such as, Why did God permit this? Has some sin been committed? Why doesn't God heal him? Finally, Fred could take it no longer.

"I got tired of facing people all the time and started to withdraw. People at the church didn't really know what was going on within me. I would preach on Sundays and that was it. I would just do my job."

Within a short time, these feelings began to affect Fred's family life as well.

"Even though I loved my wife and little boy, I just withdrew. When I would come home, I wouldn't speak to my wife. We just stopped talking. We would eat in silence. Sometimes I wouldn't even eat or come home for meals. I wouldn't even tell anyone where I was at."

Eventually, after about six months, Fred reached a point where he knew he had to do something. He reviewed his options and then made a decision.

"I could have left my wife. I had opportunities to have an affair but God watched over me. Finally, I called the board of the church together. I told them, 'Men, I've got a problem. I need your help.' They gathered around me and prayed for me. From that time on things started getting better. Everything didn't change at once, but little by little I was able to come out of myself again."

Christians are not immune from crises. Yet faith in God can and does make a difference. Fred's faith helped him to remain faithful to his wife. Not only was it a difficult time for Fred, but for his wife as well. Recognizing the struggle in Fred's life, she remained supportive of him as she placed her trust in God. Over time and with the help of friends, they were able to work through the problem.

The study of Farrell and Rosenberg indicated that those individuals who achieved a higher degree of personal integration in young adulthood were less likely to experience a crisis in mid-life. Related to this was the finding that men from lower socio-economic levels were more likely to experience feelings of alienation later in life.

Young men are able to transcend present difficulties by hoping that the future will be better. However, as they move into mid-life, this hope is likely to dissipate if they feel trapped in an unfolding pattern of events over which they have no control. Farrell and Rosenberg noted that these individuals begin to experience their poverty and lack of power and status as the defining reality of their lives. The result is a sense of bitter alienation with little hope of any positive changes occurring in the future.

This does not mean that mid-life crises are limited to those in lower socio-economic groups. Nor does it mean that those individuals are doomed to a life of trauma and misery. As noted above, a crisis can develop through the interaction of a number of forces in a person's life, some of which are beyond personal control.

It is not uncommon for a middle-aged adult to experience feelings of displacement or disorganization. The rapidly changing nature of our society constantly forces us to adapt to new circumstances. Most of the time, we are able to adjust without major disruptions in our lives. However, when a number of significant changes occur in a person's life all at once, it can easily create feelings of being off-balance. This can lead to self-examination, questions concerning the future, feelings of uncertainty, and concerns about personal security and meaning. Faith can provide stability during these periods as it did in the life of Pam Wilburn.

Pam Wilburn, Age Forty

Pam Wilburn was raised in church and made a confession of faith at the age of six. During her teen-aged years she began to have questions about God and found herself "on the fence."

"I reached a point where I didn't know what I believed or what I should believe. When I was eighteen, I went to Bible college hoping to find answers, but I didn't."

Pam dropped out of school and was soon married. She remained uncommitted concerning her relationship with God and totally ceased her participation in church. New concerns arose, however, after she became a parent.

"After our son came our marriage relationship changed. We began to have problems. I realized that I had to have something to give my son. Looking for help I began to seek the Lord.

"There was a group of women in our neighborhood who had a Bible study. I joined the group and started looking for intellectual proof. I even took a course at the nearby college.

"I finally gave in and started back to the Christian church. I didn't like it, but I kept going."

As Pam's family problems grew worse, she began to depend more upon God for strength.

"I began to search the Bible for answers to our marriage problems. I felt miserable at times, but I followed God's Word in what it had to say about marriage and children."

Suddenly, without warning, Pam's husband became ill. He was diagnosed as having cancer and died when Pam was thirty-seven. Pam's faith provided her with new strength to face his death and her uncertain future.

"I don't know how I would have made it without faith in God. It carried me through that time."

After her husband's death, Pam found herself responsible for guiding a teen-aged son and for trying to make a living. She returned to college hoping to prepare for a new career. Once again, she was trying to sort out God's will for her life. She was sensitive to the fact that her son would only be home for a few more years, then he, too, would be leaving. Pam was experiencing a major transition, yet her faith gave her a sense of stability, purpose and hope.

Transition periods, like those experienced by Fred Linder and Pam Wilburn, may last a few months or several years. They require us to alter our life structure in order to adequately cope with changing realities that may include a crisis experience. Whether or not a crisis actually takes place is related to a variety of factors including to what extent the individual has developed a sense of identity and integration, and how much one feels trapped in a set of circumstances beyond his or her control. We have seen that faith in God can make a difference in how we respond to overwhelming difficulties. In addition, we must never underestimate the power of loved ones and a supportive community in helping to weather a personal storm.

Should we expect to experience a mid-life crisis? No one can answer this question for us. We can expect, however, that at some point in time, the conditions conducive for a personal crisis are likely to develop in our lives and in the lives of our families. The ultimate question becomes, how will we respond to these circumstances and to whom can we turn for help in our hour of need? Faith in God can make a difference.

Summary

Important faith issues continued to surface during the forties. These issues were frequently related to children leaving home, the husband-wife relationship, caring for elderly parents, rethinking one's future, and a heightened awareness of death. Discerning God's will became a concern if a major disruption or change occurred in a person's life. Both men and women sought direction from God during the forties, but in general men tended to feel more unsettled during this period than did women. Important faith responses included meeting personal needs, trusting in God, reading the Bible, having a reason to live and particularly for women, relying upon the sustaining power of God. There were few intellectual concerns about faith. For the most part, those had been settled earlier in life.

Several of those interviewed became Christians during their forties. For many, marital difficulties led them to seek God. For others, it was an accumulation of life problems. A friend, one's spouse or a television program were often responsible for leading these individuals to Christ. Past memories of attending church as a child were also an important contributing factor in their conversion.

Like any period of life, middle age, which is frequently introduced by the age forty transition, has its own unique challenges and crises. When put in perspective, however, it can be a time of both high achievement and personal growth. The middle-aged person has a better grasp of reality and the experience needed to cope with a complex and changing environment. Serving as a bridge between two generations, the middle-aged adult is often in positions of leadership in both business and civic organizations. Yet feelings of responsibility may also be accompanied by an awareness that time is slipping away and whatever else that is to be accomplished in one's lifetime must be done now, otherwise, the chance may never come again. One begins to think in terms of How much time is left? rather than How old am I? The words of Job become a stark reality:

> Man born of woman is of few days and full of trouble. He springs up like
> a flower and whithers away; like a fleeting shadow, he does not endure.
> (Job 14:1–2)

In the next chapter we will explore the development and expression of
faith in the second half of middle age, the decade of the fifties.

10

The Fifties and Early Sixties

Fiftieth anniversaries are symbolized by gold. They represent a special milestone in careers, marriages, and in individual lives. There is something significant about turning fifty, and in certain respects, this decade of life is a golden era. Men are likely to be at the pinnacle of their careers; women may now find the time and opportunity to explore and to develop areas of their own lives which have been neglected in the past. Family income is likely to be at its peak with expenses on the decline after the children have left home. Yet like any period of life, turbulence can erupt as well.

The transition into the sixties represents another milestone. A person officially becomes a "senior citizen." Still, many people would rather ignore that distinction because it makes them feel old. The fact that our society places a premium upon youth makes many individuals want to avoid any vestige of appearing to be elderly.

Many of the faith issues that were present in the forties also extend into this period of life. However, certain distinct developmental tasks and issues related to this period are less prominent during the forties. During the forties, middle age is just beginning, but by the fifties, a person is clearly established in middle adulthood. For many, the last child will not leave home until sometime during this period. Couples with children are likely to become grandparents during this time if they have not already done so in their forties. Personal health concerns are likely to increase with greater attention upon chronic problems. This may also lead to a heightened awareness of aging and of the nearness of death. For many others, retirement and old age will not even be considered as primary issues. They will feel like they are in the prime of life with important goals and tasks yet to be accomplished.

The faith responses of trusting in God, relying upon his sustaining power, and believing that he will answer prayer—all prominent concerns during the thirties and into the forties—were also of central importance for both men and women during the fifties. The expression and development of faith continued to be affected by family life, career, and health concerns.

Laura Bauman and Ruth Stillman both arrived at a new level of trust in God during their early fifties. The death of relatives had led Laura Bauman to a more mature faith. Ruth Stillman, like many others, became a Christian during her forties as the result of marital problems. After her divorce at the age of forty-nine, she entered the fifties with a new dependency on and trust in God. Both Laura and Ruth felt that their relationship with God was something that could only come with age and experience.

Laura Bauman, Age Fifty

Born in 1932, Laura Bauman was an only child until she was twelve. When she was ten she began working in her father's store and she grew to feel that she was reared in an adult world. Laura's family attended a Baptist church and her grandfather was a Baptist minister. However, as a young child she did not find church to be an enjoyable part of her life.

"We had a very strict household. There were always a lot of 'can't do's.' I couldn't play, for example, on Sunday afternoon; Sunday was to be a quiet day.

"When I was about eight, there was a revival at the church. It was hell, fire, and damnation. I made a profession of faith but it didn't mean anything. Over the years I became hostile to that type of preaching."

As a teen-ager, Laura became a Christian through Youth for Christ. During high school she felt insecure and began dating Pete who would eventually become her husband. When Laura decided to attend the state university after graduating, she developed a serious conflict with her parents. They felt that the school was immoral. Laura felt slighted by her parents, but she had always done what they had told her to do.

Shortly after that, Laura married Pete and things went from bad to worse. During their first year of marriage, both she and Pete became ill and were hospitalized. Having little money and no health insurance they became dependent upon their parents for help. Later, after becoming a parent, Laura found herself socially isolated. Together she and Pete struggled financially just to make ends meet.

During that period in her life, Laura's involvement in church dwindled to almost nothing. It was not until her thirties that faith began to play an important role in her life again. The major turning point came with the death of her parents when Laura was in her late thirties.

"In the 1960s my faith began to mature more. When your world begins to fall apart, or your loved ones go, you have to hold on to something.

"My mother died of cancer in 1968. Less than two years later my father also died of cancer. Four months after that my brother-in-law was killed in an accident and then I had major surgery.

"In 1974 my grandmother died. For four years she had lived as a vegetable. It was hard for me to visit her. All these things affect us for better or worse. I realized we all age. We all go through illnesses and eventually death."

Laura felt that through those experiences she had become a more mature Christian.

"My faith is stronger today than it was ten years ago. I've come to see God as a God of love. He has a plan for me. I don't always follow it, though. I don't question God as much now. I have a better understanding of 'why.' It's part of God's plan. As you become more mature you become more realistic about your goals."

In a span of six years, Laura Bauman lost her mother, father, brother-in-law, and grandmother. She then had major surgery. All of this brought her to the realization that she, too, would eventually die. Through that experience, Laura felt her faith became more mature. She was more aware of God's love.

Ruth Stillman also felt that her relationship with God had matured because of life's problems. Faith in God had given her power to live when she was ready to end it all.

Ruth Stillman, Age Fifty-three

In 1968 Ruth Stillman was ready to commit suicide. She was having severe marriage problems and had just learned that her husband was having an affair. She made plans to drown herself but could not follow through with it because of the children. The next day she saw a minister and made a new commitment to Jesus Christ.

"I always thought that things would get better, but they didn't. Finally, there seemed to be no answer. That was when I had my first real experience with God."

Although Ruth's marriage continued to hold together, she and her husband grew further apart. In 1978 they were finally divorced. From 1968–1978, Ruth's faith helped to sustain her marital commitment. After the divorce, she felt a change had occurred in her faith.

"I wanted to keep our marriage together. The Lord worked in dreams to show me how I wasn't trusting him. A scripture would come to my mind to help me. It was a moment-by-moment thing. I had a deep dependence on the Lord.

"Since the divorce it has been a weird time. I never believed we would be divorced. Since then, even though I still have faith, I have withdrawn from people and from God. I don't want to get close to people because I'm afraid of being hurt. That has rubbed off on my faith. The constant awareness of the presence of God is not there. The faith is still there, but I go about my daily business more independent than before."

Ruth found herself facing issues related to her career, family, and age.

"I am now having to make decisions about what to do. My oldest son wants me to move to be closer to him. But should I leave my job and sell my home? I'm also trying to establish an adult relationship with my youngest son. He's not comfortable talking to me about personal decisions."

Issues related to health and mortality had also become more important to Ruth.

"My youngest brother had a heart attack recently. It's been scary. It makes me think a little bit about my own death. I'm also dealing with my mother's aging. I can see her health failing and it makes me worry about mine."

Since Ruth had first become a Christian, she had witnessed a significant change in her faith.

"Maturing as a Christian is a process regardless of your age. The older you are, the more you'll have experienced things that will help you grow. Young Christians have never had their faith tested. My faith is different today than when I first believed. It's more mature. I just don't believe because it says so in the Bible. I've seen God work in my life. That's the difference.''

As long as we face the future, there are choices to be made. None of us can escape that reality. At age fifty-three, Ruth Stillman was struggling with important decisions that would affect her future. On the one hand, Ruth had some sense of security. She had a good job and felt reasonably settled in her own home. Yet, on the other hand, she knew that in a year or two her youngest son would be leaving home and she would be alone. Ruth's oldest son wanted her to move to Florida to be near him and his family. Could she risk giving up the security and stability of a job and home to make that transition at that point in her life? At the same time, her brother's heart attack and her mother's failing health also made her more aware of her own mortality. If she did not act now, she was not sure what opportunities she would have left in the future.

Since her divorce Ruth had become more independent. She was somewhat afraid to get close to people. This had also affected her relationship with God. At times she felt distant from God, yet she also felt more mature in her faith. Her relationship with God went beyond her feelings because she had seen him work in her life in the past.

Whereas an awareness of aging begins in the thirties and becomes more prominent in the forties, it is most strongly present in the fifties. The reality of death and a new understanding of time helps to strip away illusions and modify dreams that were present in early adulthood. These issues affect both feelings of self-worth as well as career. At age fifty-seven, Raymond Freemont, who was a minister, thought a lot more about his own mortality and remaining years.

Raymond Freemont, Age Fifty-seven

Raymond Freemont was married in 1945, shortly after he graduated from college. He found the first years of the pastorate to be difficult. Concerning them, Raymond commented, ''I was too frightened by the responsibility of living to be concerned with faith.''

After he became more established, Raymond's faith continued on a steady keel until his early forties. At that time, the church he was serving embarked on a new building program. Raymond felt increased stress and tension. The new building was slowed down by a shortage of funds. There were times when Raymond felt like leaving, but he managed to see the new facility completed. By the age of fifty-seven, he had become much more aware of his own mortality.

"I think a lot about the fact that my life is nearly over. My good years are behind me with respect to my health. There are still certain things I haven't accomplished. I see so many people die on the vine. I don't want that to happen to me."

Hopefully, none of us want to "die on the vine." And at fifty-seven, Raymond had many good years still ahead of him. Countless stories could be told of men and women who began interesting and successful careers later in life. Albert Spencer, who was fifty-eight was just beginning a new pastorate when I interviewed him. He was enthusiastic about life and he had a vision for the congregation. His health, though, was a reminder that he was entering later adulthood. In certain respects, Albert's health was more of a concern to his wife than it was to him.

Albert and Flora Spencer,
Ages Fifty-eight and Fifty-five

Albert Spencer had open heart surgery when he was fifty-seven. Even though his wife Flora had trusted God to watch over him, nevertheless, she found it to be a time of crisis.

"The crisis of my faith has been his health. I have faith in God, but also an inner fear of his heart. It's easier to accept things for yourself. You don't really know how the other person is feeling and your feelings go out to them."

Reflecting on his life, Albert had seen his faith grow in stages.

"I was raised in a Christian home and was saved when I was nine years old. My faith became stronger once I left home. After I left home, I had to make my own decisions so I had to depend upon God more. My faith grew once we went into the full-time ministry. At first I didn't always have faith that he would supply all our needs. Then I learned that he was our Heavenly Father."

Reflecting on her own life, Flora felt more in control of her emotions than she had earlier in life.

"I'm not as emotionally up and down as I used to be. I'm more stable emotionally about things."

Albert commented that he felt less rigid than he had as a young man.

"In the beginning I wanted to make people perfect. Now I accept people more the way they are and give them time to mature."

Albert had seen his faith develop in stages. He expressed the same responses that we have seen consistently. After he first left home, he had to become more independent and determine what he believed as well as to make his own decisions. When he first began to work he found it difficult to trust God, relying instead, upon himself. Later his faith became more directed toward God. Also, over time he became flexible and more accepting of people that were different from him. As Albert began to have health problems, it became a crisis for his wife. While she had faith in God, she also feared that her husband might die of heart problems.

One of the greatest fears that married women have during their fifties is that their husband may have a heart attack. The greatest stress that most individuals ever experience is the loss of their spouse. While in his late fifties, Matt Parson's wife became seriously ill. Her health problems had an impact on the expression of Matt's faith.

Matt Parson, Age Fifty-eight

Though Matt Parson grew up in a Christian home, he found himself drifting away from God while he was in the army during World War II. After the war he was married. When he became a parent he decided that the family should go to church for the sake of his child, but it meant little to him.

"We went to church but I wasn't a Christian. I'd run around with the boys. After work, I'd go down to the tavern and drink three or four beers.

"One night I came home and my wife was sitting there with our little boy. He was sick and had a fever. She said, 'I've been trying to get a hold of you. If this is the way a Christian acts, then I don't want any part of it.' Right then and there it just hit me. I knew I had to do something about God in my life."

Over the years Matt became a respected member and leader in the church where he attended. His faith in God had helped him face several difficulties in his life.

"I think different things come into your life to test your faith. Your faith has to be changing all the time. It's got to become stronger.

"I went through a time of testing in 1966. I went in for a routine check-up and they found I had a bad valve in my heart. Then I got sick in 1972 and was in the hospital on two different occasions. Both times it was my heart. But after all was said and done, they never had to do anything to it. I ended up having a gall bladder operation instead."

Matt's most difficult test was still in progress, however. During the past year, his wife had become critically ill and there was little he could do to help her.

"My wife is going through a very bad time right now. My faith has got to be strong because of her. Last December the doctors found out she had cancer. She had a hysterectomy in January. After that she had a herniated disc in her back and she's never recovered. She hasn't been to church for months."

Matt felt that his wife's illness had caused him to have stronger faith in God, although there were some things he did not understand.

"I'm only human. Sure, there are times I question why things happen. But there's a reason for it—to make our faith stronger. I won't say that my faith doesn't waver from time-to-time. But as I hold out, I know things will go my way. The strongest Christian living will sometimes wonder what's happening."

Concerning grief and trials, the Apostle Peter wrote: "These have come so that your faith—of greater worth than gold, which perishes even though refined by fire—may be proved genuine and may result in praise, glory and honor when Jesus Christ is revealed" (1 Pet. 1:7). Genuine faith endures times of testing. That is not true because the individual grits his or her teeth and tries harder; rather the strength to endure comes from God. As Peter has written, "Through faith [you] are shielded by God's power . . . " (1 Pet. 1:5). God's grace is sufficient for every situation.

Individuals in their fifties are likely to have their faith tested as the result of health problems. Women are more likely to become widows during this period than they were earlier in life. Frequently, when this does occur, the woman can expect to live several more decades. That was the case for Elizabeth Barnes who became a widow at age sixty.

Elizabeth Barnes, Age Sixty

Elizabeth Barnes was married during World War II right after she finished college. One year after she was married, her husband left to fight in the war. Six weeks later, she gave birth to a son. When Robert, her husband, returned the baby was fourteen months old.

Elizabeth felt that her life unfolded in a manner that was for the most part anticipated. She and her family remained active in the church throughout her adult life. When she encountered problems, she viewed them as stepping stones to personal growth.

"My faith has always been growing. I think that a person's age, maturity, and experience helps them to understand life better. We all go through difficulties, but if we have the right attitude, the experience can strengthen us. It helps us to help others."

The single greatest trial of Elizabeth's life was the death of her mother. Although it occurred seventeen years ago, when Elizabeth was forty-three, it still affected her.

"Father died when I was fourteen. All my sisters were already married and that left my mother and me at home alone. I was always very close to her.

"When she died it was very traumatic, even more so than when my husband Robert died. I had feelings of guilt because she died in a nursing home. We just couldn't keep her at home.

"She never wanted to interfere in the lives of her children. I knew she wanted me to see her but it was hard to go. Later she always wanted to come home with us. She was eighty-seven when she died.

"After that I had feelings of distress. It took me about a year to work through it. I don't know if I felt guilty but I had a lot of dreams about my mother. When my husband died, I didn't dream about him for months."

Elizabeth's husband died when she was fifty-seven. Since he had been ill for sometime his death did not come as a total surprise. Afterwards the Bible, her family members, and her church have become a source of comfort to Elizabeth.

"Since Robert died I've read the Bible more. In times of stress I have learned to turn to God and the Bible. I've also been affirmed by my church family. I relate well to my children. I don't need their permission to do anything."

Elizabeth found pleasure in reflecting on the creative nature of her family. Not only did she enjoy thinking about the past, but she also looked forward to the future.

"I had a very creative husband and family. My husband made all types of things including the stained glass windows of our church. He was constantly involved in hobbies like woodworking. Our children picked up on this creativity, including my musical interests.

"Since Robert died I've written three musicals for the church. I also intend to write two books in the future. I'm a people person, but I also enjoy being alone. I feel good about my life. I would like to go to Europe. I don't have any desire to marry again, but I would like to be asked out.

I don't know many single men my age, though.''

Since her husband's death, Bible reading became a more important part of Elizabeth's life. She felt that a person's attitude was the key to serving God and enjoying life. Although Elizabeth was significantly affected by the death of her mother and husband, she maintained a proactive stance toward life, which reflected the way that she had embraced life during earlier years.

Most people do not experience radical personality changes during any period of life. Who we are and who we are becoming is in part a reflection of who we have been. The biblical principle that we reap what we sow pertains to every aspect of life. Elizabeth Barnes viewed trials as stepping stones to personal growth. She attempted to utilize the lessons that she had learned from life to help others. That is a reflection of mature faith. In his second letter to the Corinthians, Paul instructed his readers that God "comforts us in all our troubles, so that we can comfort those in any trouble with the comfort we ourselves have received from God" (1:4).

Toward the end of the fifties and into the early sixties, retirement becomes more of an issue for men. People retire for many different reasons. At sixty-three, Bert Good retired in order to achieve some personal goals. He viewed later adulthood as a period where he could devote more time to serving God.

Bert Good, Age Sixty-three

During his twenties and thirties, Bert Good found his life consumed by his career. A chain smoker and a heavy drinker, he was also physically abusive to his wife. When Bert was forty-one, his wife became a Christian. Later a minister visited them at their home. Bert's own life was in a state of turmoil and he, too, began to seek God.

"I had a hunger for God. I went from one church to another seeking something. I became concerned about my career and family.

"All of a sudden the Lord came into my heart. I quit smoking. From there I started working in a church, but I wasn't grounded enough. My wife and I weren't stable.''

As Bert's marriage continued to deteriorate, he felt his faith begin to slip.

"After our youngest child was born, my wife and I stopped all sexual relations. This lasted over a year. Then she started having an affair. My faith collapsed. I wasn't as strong as I thought I was. I started looking around myself for a woman to sleep with.''

Shortly thereafter, Bert and his wife were divorced. Bert started attending Parents Without Parents hoping to find a sexual relationship. However, at one of the meetings he met a Christian woman who led him back to God. Eventually they were married but Bert still encountered difficulties in his life.

''I had a strong desire to be close to God, but alcohol had taken over my life. I couldn't get rid of it. Even though I was drinking I would testify about the Lord at work. One Saturday I walked into this tavern and there sat this guy I had witnessed to. I felt that I had lost my testimony. I heard God say to me, 'You have to be hot or cold. If you're lukewarm I'll spit you out of my mouth.' That scared me. I knew I had to make a decision.''

That event became the turning point in Bert's Christian life. With the support of his second wife he was able to face his problem with alcohol. Sensing that he only had so much time left to live, at sixty-three Bert decided to retire. He wanted to spend the rest of his life serving God and doing something that he felt was useful. Bert perceived that much of his earlier life had been wasted. At the time of this interview, Bert was working as a scout leader with the boys in his church. He wanted his faith to be put to action.

Summary

The period of the fifties and the early sixties is a time of great variation and diversity related to adult development. Many experience increased responsibilities and higher status in their careers. Others realize, however, that certain career goals will never be accomplished and must learn to accept those realities.

Health can have a dramatic impact on how a person embraces life during this period. For some, chronic health problems begin to emerge, creating new boundaries which limit personal activities and thwart goals. The declining health of one's spouse can also create a heavy emotional burden which tests one's faith. More women become widowed during this time span than in earlier years. This is especially true for women who have married older men. Retirement also begins to become more of an issue for men.

Trust in God must constantly be renegotiated throughout life. New issues continue to emerge which test faith. Yet God's past faithfulness provides a foundation for continued trust later in life. The longer a person is a Christian there seems to be less need to seek answers as to why things happen. That does not mean, however, that questions are not raised. It does imply that genuine trust looks beyond the circumstances to an eternal God who knows the end from the beginning. Mature faith is reflected by using personal difficulties as stepping stones to personal growth.

> And we know that in all things God works for the good of those who love him, who have been called according to his purpose. (Rom. 8:28)

11
The Mid- To Late Sixties

Many people perceive later adulthood to begin around sixty-five. This is probably because for the past generation retirement took place at or near that age. In a society that glamorizes youth and vitality, later adulthood has become a period of life which many would rather ignore. Old age has received more than its share of "bad press." Unfortunately, there are more myths about this stage of life than of any other single period of the life cycle.

An individual's age is not a good indicator of physical condition, mental outlook, or personal character. There is tremendous diversity among the elderly in terms of spiritual, physical, social, economic, and psychological condition. It would be a mistake to treat those in old age as a homogeneous group because they simply are not.[1] Before examining the development and expression of faith during later adulthood, it will be helpful to review the more salient characteristics of this period of life.

Later Adulthood

Later adulthood covers the period from the early sixties until death. Naturally there are significant differences between someone who is sixty-three and someone eighty-nine, but the same is true for the age range in early or middle adulthood. There are vast distinctions between an eighteen-year-old and a person thirty-eight.

Like other eras in the life cycle, later adulthood has its own unique tasks and issues. One major task of this stage is to review past accomplishments and failures and to accept the realities which have transpired throughout one's life. Some may find that difficult to do, especially if important dreams and goals were never realized. Others, however, may find gratification in past accomplishments or take pride in the lives of their children or grandchildren. Individuals respond to the past in extremely different ways. For some it may lead to depression or anger. Others, though, may recall their earlier years with a great sense of joy. We must remember, that who we become later in life is shaped by who we are today and who we were yesterday. "Becoming" is a lifelong process. Those who are bitter and depressed for any extended period are likely to remain in that condition unless at some point they choose to change. But to change requires personal effort and frequently entails pain. Even though they are unhappy some people find it easier to live with themselves than to risk change.

One important aspect of later adulthood is that one major need or problem can have a rippling effect throughout the individual's life. For example, Harris notes that a health problem can affect income, transportation, housing, employment, and vulnerability to crime.[2] Retirement can bring about a decline in income affecting lifestyle or self-esteem. The loss of a spouse can produce great trauma and intense feelings of loneliness and affect nearly every other aspect of life.

The Myths of Aging

Older people do face unique problems and challenges. Yet too frequently the elderly are stereotyped in a way that is out of touch with reality. Robert Butler has discussed a number of myths which are popularly used to describe old age.[3] Six of these myths are described below.

1. *Myth of aging.* Because people age at different rates and in different ways, it is incorrect to categorize people by age alone. Yet the elderly are often portrayed as a homogeneous group.

2. *Myth of unproductivity.* Older adults can remain productive in work, community and family life given a supportive environment and the absence of major health problems. Unfortunately, many believe that being

old means being unproductive. That is not true.

3. *Myth of disengagement.* Some people believe that the elderly want to withdraw from life and be left alone; however, that is false. Social interaction is important for people of all ages.

4. *Myth of inflexibility.* Older adults are often portrayed as being inflexible and set in their ways. The ability to change and adapt has less to do with one's age, and more to do with a person's total response to life.

5. *Myth of senility.* Those in later adulthood are frequently viewed as being confused or forgetful. Yet other factors such as grief, depression, medication, malnutrition, or physical illness may account for such responses in certain individuals. Older adults experience the full range of emotional responses like everyone else. Most older adults do not become senile. Some, though, do experience irreversible brain damage, which may result in senility.

6. *Myth of serenity.* This myth projects the elderly into a fairytale world. Life is viewed as peaceful and serene. Grandma bakes cookies and Grandpa tends the garden. In reality, the elderly experience more stress than any other age group.

Unless we are careful, these myths can prejudice the way we view and respond to older adults. It is imperative that Christians understand and adequately react to the needs of the elderly. Currently, one out of every ten Americans is age sixty-five or over. By the year 2000 that number will increase to one out of eight. For years there has been an emphasis upon "youth" ministry in the church. Considering the nature of our society there needs to be an emphasis upon ministry to those in later adulthood.

Developmental Tasks of Later Adulthood

In addition to assessing and reviewing the past, other important developmental tasks are present during this era of life. Three major areas which generally surface at that time in life include retirement, health concerns, and widowhood.

Retirement. Retirement represents the single most important role change for a man in later adulthood. While some eagerly anticipate more leisure time, others resent retirement. One study has indicated that for forty percent of older persons, retirement was not their own choice.[4]

For some retirement symbolizes becoming elderly. For many it entails a significant decline in income. Harris comments that twenty-five percent of all persons over age sixty-five are considered poor or near poor according to government standards.[5] The ability to earn an adequate income after retirement is a major source of difficulty for many older people. This is of special concern once it is realized that by the year 2000 it is estimated that the average life expectancy after retirement will be approximately twenty-five years.[6] Today it is slightly over fifteen years. That is a long time to live on reduced benefits.

Retirement means more than the loss of income. Often it can mean the loss of meaningful social relationships which occurred at work. The retired person may be at a loss about what to do with his or her time. Also, the intrinsic satisfaction of work itself may leave a personal void.[7] The impact of retirement affects individuals differently. But no matter how you look at it, it is a major turning point in a person's life.

Health. Health concerns tend to increase with age. While acute health problems afflict the young, the elderly experience more chronic health concerns. A major study conducted by the National Council on Aging indicated the following highlights concerning physical health of individuals over sixty-five years of age.[8]

1. Approximately eighty-six percent of the population over age sixty-five have one or more chronic conditions.

2. Most individuals do not consider themselves to be seriously handicapped by their health problems.

3. Only one person in twenty resides in a long-term health care facility like a nursing home. Most adults live in family settings.

While the elderly do experience more health concerns than do the young or middle-aged, for the most part, they are able to compensate for these problems and lead a fairly normal and productive life. Nevertheless medical expenses and personal impairment do affect the quality of life in later adulthood.

Widowhood. The death of a spouse is the most stressful of all events, regardless of a person's age. The personal disorganization that follows widowhood usually requires a restructuring of roles and relationships. This is true for both men and women. A woman, though, is far more likely to outlive her husband than vice versa. Not only do women have a longer life expectancy, but frequently women marry older men. Thus it is probable that the husband will precede his wife in death.

The degree and nature of the disorganization that follows the death of one's spouse is affected by the age of the widow.[9] Young women with no children usually reenter the single marital category. Middle-aged women with dependent children are likely to feel the greatest loss. They experience widowhood "off-time." Often they are faced with financial hardships and concerns about career and employment. Friendships, which for the most part are likely to be with other married couples, may now seem awkward. Furthermore, these widows must not only deal with their own grief, but with that of their children as well.

Widows between the ages of fifty-five and sixty-five may also struggle financially even though they may have no children at home. They are too young for social security, and unless they have been working, they feel intimidated because of their age to enter the labor force.

Older women may feel less financial or social disorganization, but they are likely to experience extreme loneliness and isolation after the loss of their husband. Of course that is also true of an individual of any age. No matter how old the woman or man, the loss of one's spouse is a traumatic event. It is most likely to occur, though, during later adulthood. The average woman can expect to live 18.5 years after the loss of her husband. For a man it is 13.5 years after the death of his wife.[10]

Widowhood is often followed by certain psychosomatic symptoms.[11] These may include headaches, nervousness, loss of appetite, upset stomach, trouble sleeping, dizziness, and rapid heart beat. The widow may feel that her identity has been shattered and feels uncomfortable in former social roles. At the same time, she is forced to become more independent and may find roles thrust upon her, like maintaining the car, which had previously been done by the husband. These new roles and responsibilities may create additional tension. Generally, numerous changes occur and it takes time for the widow to restructure her life in order to adequately cope with her new life situation. According to Lopata, the most desolate of all widows are those who feel that they have no pleasurable and meaningful relationships.[12]

The Development and Expression of Faith

During the mid- to late sixties, the expression of faith was very much related to health concerns, family life, and the awareness that time was running out. Again, as in earlier periods, believing that God would meet personal needs, trusting in God, and reading the Bible were all important expressions of faith. This was true for both men and women. Additional faith responses also surfaced during this period in relationship to changing life circumstances. For men, there was an increased focus upon assurance or knowing that after they died, their destiny (heaven) was assured. For women, the responses of "knowing God is there" and "Bible reading" became more important. Furthermore, these two responses were very much related. This was particularly true for widows who now felt alone. Reading the Bible provided not only comfort but an increased sense that God was present. As Edith Reynolds (age eighty-one) said back in the first chapter of this book,

"When you're alone you don't have someone to talk things over with before you go to bed or when you wake up. I talk to God. The Lord is just there. Many nights I'll quote the whole Ninety-first Psalm before I go to sleep."

In the remainder of this chapter, we will examine the expression of faith in the lives of two men and two women between the ages of sixty-five and seventy.

Elaine Whitt, Age Sixty-seven

Elaine Whitt became a Christian when she was fifty. Though she had been reared in a Christian home, Elaine had always felt that something was missing in her life.

"I became born again through a Bible study when I was fifty years old. I was looking for something. I received an invitation to a tea which was also a Bible study. At that time I was smoking and I knew it wasn't good for me. I said, 'God, I know you are real. I want to quit smoking and I don't want to gain weight.' Right then and there I asked him into my life."

Twelve years later, at the age of sixty-two, Elaine became a widow. Her husband's death affected her own relationship with God.

"When my husband died it was hard for me to pray, especially for others. I could pray for myself though. The grief lasted a long time. It's just within the last year that I have been able to pray. Now I'm starting to get new interests like going to garage sales. I'm finding more things to keep myself busy."

Elaine's mother, who was still alive and living in a nursing home, was a source of major concern. Being an only child, Elaine felt responsible for the welfare of her mother. Facing her mother's condition had helped Elaine rethink her own commitment and responsibilities as a Christian.

"Several years ago mother had a car accident. She lived for a week and I was expecting her to die at any moment. Then she had a stroke, but she kept on living. All along I was preparing for her death and when she didn't die, I had to prepare for her living.

"I had a hard time putting her in a nursing home. I cleaned her house out of fifty years of possessions. Here's where I questioned God, 'Why do you let her live like this?' I pleaded for six months and then realized he wasn't going to take her.

"God had something to teach me—patience. I had to learn to face up to life. I've learned that I can go into that nursing home and serve others. I can give a cup of water and bring joy to people.

"My mother's been there now for three years. She's the only family I have. I go to the nursing home and witness to others. It's been a joyful time even though I've seen a lot of suffering there."

Although Elaine's faith had drawn her closer to God, she still wrestled with being alone.

"I struggle with being content in the state I'm in. I have faith that God will take care of me for I'm truly alone. After my husband died, I bought a dog. She's like a person to me. I never had a pet before. She means so much to me. I think about my future and am trying to prepare for my own death. I want to be ready, to know that I'll be with Christ."

Even though Elaine thought about her own death, she was still in good health and active in her church. Rather than feeling angry or depressed about her situation, she sought to serve God and to live the remainder of her life in a way that was pleasing to him.

"I'm accepting my life as it is. I know that God knows where I am and this is where he wants me right now. I still think of myself as young. The only thing that I would do different, if I had my life to live over, is to become a Christian earlier in life."

Although Elaine Whitt did not become a Christian until age fifty, her childhood background in the church helped to pave the way for her conversion. Prompted by health concerns and trying to fill a void in her life, Elaine found Christ through a neighborhood Bible study. Later the death of her husband and her mother's failing health brought her to a point of increased trust in and dependency upon God. At the age of sixty-seven, Elaine was learning to be a faithful servant, to face up to life, and at the same time, to prepare for death.

Lena Huss, Age Sixty-six

In reviewing her life, Lena Huss also found herself rethinking her priorities and commitments in the face of death. Yet she had discovered that God was always present in times of need.

"I have found that God is always faithful at testing periods. He either does a miracle or changes your outlook.

"My faith was tested the most when I was raising the children. You have to lean more heavily on the Lord for wisdom during those times.

"Now that the children are grown and gone, I'm trying to take time to evaluate my life. I'm realizing just how short life is. Are the things we're doing valuable? I want to be dedicated to the right things."

In particular, these concerns were prompted in Lena's life by the death of loved ones.

"The older you get, you realize more strongly you can't take one thing with you. You start seeing the death of your friends and parents. My brother died last year. He had never been sick. He was a millionaire, but when he was in that coffin, he didn't have one thing in his hands.

"There will come a day when we all will pass off the scene. We might work hard for things, but we can't take them with us. Only spiritual things will remain."

Jesus said, "What good will it be for a man if he gains the whole world, yet forfeits his soul?" (Matt. 16:26). The drive to accumulate material possessions can take control of our lives. Furthermore, it plunges us into ruin and destruction. The scriptures warn us that "some people, eager for money, have wandered from the faith and pierced themselves with many griefs" (1 Tim. 6:10). On the other hand we are reminded, "godliness with contentment is great gain. For we brought nothing into the world, and we can take nothing out of it. But if we have food and clothing, we will be content with that" (1 Tim. 6:6-8).

Owning material possessions became far less important to Lena Huss the longer she lived. She wanted to redirect her life and energies in ways that counted. Her brother's death made her realize that we can take nothing with us. The only thing that endures is that which is done for God. The most important task for Lena was to remain faithful to him.

When a person does become a widow or widower in later adulthood, it is much more common for men to remarry than women. For the most part, that is true because there are fewer single men than there are single women. For example, beyond age eighty there are five single women for every single man. Harold Robinson became a widower when he was sixty-six. He remarried two years later.

Harold Robinson, Age Sixty-eight

Harold Robinson became a Christian as an eighteen-year-old on December 18, 1932. He remembered the date well because it was his parents' wedding anniversary.

"I was laying in bed praying when a vision appeared to me. Jesus was standing there in person and said, 'I'll never forsake thee or leave thee.' "

Over the years that vision had become a source of strength and comfort to Harold.

"My faith has increased over the years. I know where I'd go if I were called away the next minute. Faith is positive assurance. That vision has bolstered me. It gave me the feeling that I had something that I never had before. There were times when I would get down in the dumps, but the Holy Spirit would bring back my memory of that vision and I'd serve him."

Several years ago Harold's first wife died. Though he has remarried, her death had made him realize that his days are limited.

"I realize that the end is near. The time is short. I realize that more now. I don't have anything in particular left to do—just bring more lost people into the Kingdom. Before my wife died, she said, 'Make sure I meet the kids in heaven.' I'm not worrying about tomorrow. I just worry about today."

Harold had fallen and hurt his back. That prevented him from getting out of the house as much as he would have liked to. Yet he was still taking courses and working for a college degree. Concerning his faith, Harold commented, "Faith isn't what you get from God. It's what you do in response to God. It's doing what's right."

Even though Harold knew that death was near, he was not planning to sit passively by and wait for it to come. His back problems limited his activity, but he was still taking courses and planned to graduate from college. The most important thing in his life, though, was to be ready to meet God, and to help other people enter the Kingdom of God as well.

John Leighland, Age Sixty-nine

John Leighland grew up in the United Church of Christ. Although he attended church, he never felt close to God. After he was married he and his wife attended a Baptist church where John came under conviction.

"I felt scared. When the minister gave the invitation I went forward."

Later, John felt that a dramatic change had occurred in his life. Before, he was hesitant to speak about God in public, but after his conversion he noticed a change in his attitude.

"I had a new boldness to speak about the Lord. People noticed a difference in my life."

John's faith is what gave his life stability and meaning.

"I can stand on the Word. My faith keeps me on my feet. I had a heart attack twelve years ago. The doc wanted me to have a test but I said, 'The Lord made me and he can take care of me. I don't need it!' "

Neither did John feel that his retirement had slowed him down any.

"I thought that retirement would be a change, but it hasn't. I've got a workshop and a garden that keep me busy. I work harder now than I did when I was working. The Lord has met all of our needs."

The only significant task that John felt was left in his life was to look forward to meeting Christ. He enjoyed his leisure time and felt that God was meeting all of his needs. Faith in God was a stablizing force in his life which helped him to cope with health problems and daily life. Death was not a major concern to John.

Summary

While most of those interviewed were conscious of the nearness of death, none expressed any fear of dying. Although a few had some regrets as they looked back over their life, most sensed God's presence in ways that led to feelings of assurance and comfort. No one expressed any goals related to career, but that did not mean that no goals existed. John Leighland felt that he was more active and worked harder after retirement than before. Harold Robinson was completing a college degree and Lena Huss was actively traveling across the United States with her husband who was a retired minister. Elaine Whitt had dedicated herself to serve God at a nursing home. Others were involved in different activities.

There are many misconceptions about later adulthood. Given the opportunity, older adults will make valuable contributions to church, family and community life. My interviews indicated, that of all age groups, these individuals were perhaps the most conscious of God's presence and they earnestly desired to serve Him. They truly attempted to translate faith into action.

The righteous will live by faith. (Rom. 1:17)

12
The Seventies and Beyond

Earl Gaines had just returned from deep-sea fishing off the coast of Acapulco. He and his fiancee had a wonderful time shopping and sight-seeing in that famous Mexican resort. Earl, eighty-three, was already making plans for his honeymoon.

Not everyone who is eighty-three would like to go deep-sea fishing, even if they were able. As we have seen throughout this book, there are vast differences between people of the same age. Every human being is unique; yet, we also have many similarities. During this late period of later adulthood, several factors surface which affect most people within this age range. Health concerns are one of the greatest factors affecting the quality of life. Even though Earl Gaines was actively engaged in life, he also suffered from diabetes, arthritis and poor vision. He could no longer drive at night. Such a decrease in mobility can impair social interaction or create feelings of being trapped and isolated. Most people over seventy suffer from chronic health problems. That is not to say, however, that they are out of commission. For example, when was the last time you were in Acapulco? Only five percent of older adults end up in a long-term health care facility.

Ultimately, though, death faces every person who makes it this far in the life cycle. As we noted earlier, life progresses in only one direction—from birth to death. For many, death is an unpleasant topic. It is seldom a topic of conversation at dinner parties, for example. Perhaps that is due to the fact that the average person has little direct contact with death. Throughout most of history, however, that was not the case. High infant mortality rates, famines, epidemics, wars, and inadequate medical care made exposure to death a common experience.[1]

Death has also been removed from a religious orientation to one that has increasingly become governed by science, business, politics, and institutionalization. The act of dying can become a complicated legal process. For many dying has become a technological process. It has also been removed further away from the family and becomes ''managed'' more by doctors and other hospital personnel.[2] Today, approximately seventy to eighty percent of all deaths occur in institutional settings. These institutions frequently segregate death from the rest of society leaving many individuals to die alone in an antiseptic atmosphere.[3] Furthermore, since death is so distasteful within our society, those with a high risk of mortality, which include the elderly, tend to be isolated.[4]

It is common to associate death with fear and pain. Studies have indicated that the elderly actually express fewer fears of death than do the young.[5] However, that does not mean that there are no fears. Like other life circumstances, people face death in different ways. Some are ready to die during old age while others are not. Readiness for death depends on how satisfactorily the individual has worked through specific spiritual, psychological, and social tasks.[6] If tasks related to these areas have not been successfully addressed, that may actually create more stress than physical ailments.[7] Nevertheless, the fear of death apparently tends to diminish with age.

Awareness of death's imminency is not directly related to age. It is more tied to how long one feels he or she has left to live. Naturally, those in late adulthood are more likely to be aware of the nearness of death than those who are younger. While many individuals may think about their own death when they become middle-aged, it is too abstract to affect the self like it does when death actually becomes an impending reality.[8] During middle age a person is likely to experience the death of his or her parents. During later adulthood, one's friends, brothers, sisters, and spouse die. That makes death a very personal reality. The realization comes that ''I will die too.''

Women are much more likely to die alone than are men, because they tend to become widows. They are also likely to experience loneliness later in life before they die. These feelings and life circumstances affect the development and expression of faith.

The Development and Expression of Faith

For the most part, the same faith issues were present for these individuals as for those in their late sixties. Perhaps Mildred Albright, age seventy-two, summed up one primary concern in the following way: "My faith has gotten stronger as I've gotten older. You know you don't have much time left. You've got to get close to God now or you don't get another chance later." Mr. and Mrs. Jackson, both of whom were age seventy-seven, put it this way:

Mr. Jackson: "The most important thing right now is knowing we've got an eternal home."

Mrs. Jackson: "That's all we've got to look forward to."

That is not to say that these individuals were not active and involved in life. Far from it. Yet many of the widows did feel lonely and isolated. Involvement in church activities was a very important part of their lives. This was illustrated in the life of Bess Knight.

Bess Knight, Age Seventy-nine

Bess Knight was married in 1921 when she was nineteen. Three years later she faced a crisis when her fourteen-month-old son died. Looking for help, she and her husband went to a church where they both made a commitment to Christ. They noticed an immediate change in their lives.

"We did everything the world did. But then we changed—no more playing cards or drinking. We were the only couple who didn't get a divorce among our friends."

Like millions of others, Mr. Knight was out of work during the Depression. It was a difficult time for the family. Mrs. Knight recalled the experience.

"The Depression was hard. We had two children and no work. We had to trust God more—even for our food. I remember fixing Cream of Wheat for our baby once. We hardly had any but the Lord seemed to make it go further. He always helped us."

Bess's two boys were in the service during World War II. Though they grew up in the church, they both dropped out once they left home. Later Mr. Knight had a stroke. Bess found most of her time taken up with health care until his death in 1979. During the past several years, the church had played an increasingly important role in her life.

"Since my husband died, I've had a terrible loneliness. We were married fifty-eight years and did everything together. Now I go to church and to the prayer meetings. I couldn't live without that. I have some difficulty getting to church, though."

Bess did not think much about her future. Faith was simply trusting God to meet her needs.

"I'm just believing that God will take care of me. I trust God for what I have. I could use more money but it doesn't bother me."

Bess Knight reflected many of the prominent concerns of elderly women: loneliness; living on a small income which barely allowed her to survive; and, frequently finding transportation a problem. Mrs. Knight trusted that God would take care of her. On the day I interviewed her she, escorted by her minister, was attending a statewide conference. She expressed how much it meant for her to know that someone cared enough to do that for her.

Max Springer, Age Seventy-one

In looking back over his life, Max Springer felt that he now had more time for God than he had during earlier years. He also noticed a significant difference between his present expression of faith and that of his youth. The reality of death had changed his perspective.

"I grew up in the church. Now I attend the Salvation Army. My faith is deeper and stronger now than what it used to be. Before, when you're younger, you don't have as much time for God. You've got your job and family to keep you busy.

"I worked at a foundry seven days a week, twelve to fourteen hours a day. The only day I got off was Christmas. During the Depression there were always twenty-five or thirty men waiting outside for your job. You had to do what the boss told you or you would lose your job.

"Now I realize that I don't have much time left. I'm on the other side of the hill. The only thing that counts is being close to God. God has provided for all my needs. I've got food on the table and a place to get out of the weather. God's given me good health. What more do you need? A person can be ninety and still be greedy. Greed will lead to disappointment because you'll end up with nothing."

Max Springer had struggled to earn a living most of his life. As a younger man, he did not feel he had much time for God, and his job had consumed his life. Now he felt that the only important thing was to be close to the Lord. His wife had died and he was alone. Recognizing that he could not take anything with him, he was content with what he had. He felt that God had provided for all of his needs.

Amos Clapp believed that God was blessing him more in his old age than perhaps at any other time in his life. He felt his faith in God had grown stronger over time.

Amos Clapp, Age Eighty-two

The turning point in Amos Clapp's spiritual development came in 1950 when he was in a car accident. He spent 105 days in the hospital and was on the verge of death.

"One day I just sat up and said, 'God, I'm going to serve you.' I had never been to church in my life, but I had a praying mother. That's what did it for me."

Amos began to attend a Pentecostal church which led to problems with his wife. They were divorced in 1962 when Amos was sixty-two.

"She was a hard-nosed Baptist. She would always make fun and find fault with Pentecostals. Some people say that I tried to ram it down her throat."

After the car accident, Amos was left blind in one eye. In his old age that had caused him problems, both physically and socially.

"There are a lot of things I don't see. My head's scarred from all the things I've run into. Sometimes I even run into people. They don't understand. At church they might reach out to shake my hand and I won't see them. I walk on by and they think I'm rude. It's embarrassing to me."

Amos felt that the Lord had blessed him. He believed that his faith in God was as strong as ever.

"Before I was a Christian I tried to make it, but never did. I'm more wealthy today than I ever was. I just live on my interest now. Next month I'm going to Alaska for thirty-one days. I've been to Hawaii and Jerusalem too."

Amos trusted God now because he had seen him provide for his needs earlier in life.

"One time in my business I really needed to come up with twelve hundred dollars. A man came in and bought a boat and trailer. You ask me about faith! Never stop God from blessing you. And no matter what anybody says, don't go back. He'll take care of you."

A car accident, which left Amos Clapp blind in one eye, prompted him to become a Christian when he was fifty. Twelve years later, he and his wife were divorced. While Amos regretted much of his past life, he had come to trust in God more deeply later in life. His blindness, which sometimes led to moments of embarrassment, also led to his conversion.

By the time he was eighty-two, Amos was spending time traveling and enjoying life. He was committed to trusting in God because of past experience. He remembered how God had answered prayer concerning financial needs earlier in his life. Now he felt blessed and was now able to live from his interest. His words of encouragement were, "No matter what anybody says, don't go back. He'll take care of you."

Summary

Later adulthood is a period to review and evaluate one's life. It is also a time to grow closer to God because one realizes that time is short. For some, this period of life can bring intense loneliness. Inadequate finances can create additional burdens. Health concerns become more prominent which often affect mobility and social interaction.

In terms of faith, this period of life reflects an increased awareness of God's abiding presence. Earlier, life may have been consumed with rearing children, advancing in a career, acquiring possessions, or other goals. Those things now become memories. Material possessions were unimportant to those I interviewed, although they may have been important earlier in life. There was an increased awareness that nothing could be taken to the grave, except that which had been done for God. For those who struggled financially, they did their best to adapt to their circumstances. They placed their trust in God and felt that there was little chance that their situation would change for the better in the future. The primary goal was to prepare to meet the Lord. The future was in him.

> I have fought the good fight, I have finished the race, I have kept the faith.
> (2 Tim. 4:7)

13
Faith and Adulthood

We began this study by raising questions concerning the relationship between faith and aging. One question was, As we age, how does faith in God adapt to the changing realities of life? As we have explored the various periods of the adult life cycle and the development and expression of faith, we have seen that there is a dynamic interaction between faith responses and developmental issues and tasks. That is, faith in God affects the way Christians respond to life, but life circumstances also affect the way that faith is expressed. In the remainder of this chapter we will examine the relationship of faith to critical issues and tasks that surface throughout the life cycle. Particular attention will be given to the relationship between faith and career, family life, health, death, and life transitions. The chapter will conclude by examining faith and the Kingdom of God.

Faith and Career

Work is a fundamental task of adulthood. A person works in order to live. While animals are left to instinct, Man has the unique ability to think about and plan for the future. For some, this means trying to find a "blueprint" for their life. But none exists. As Emil Brunner has noted, planning for the future is more like hacking one's way through a jungle than following a clearly delineated path.[1]

As a person enters adulthood, he or she must decide about a vocation. That does not mean that a career will or should be selected immediately. Yet one cannot escape certain fundamental questions concerning existence. One of these questions is, What am I going to do with my life? Man is driven by this question. A decision must be made.

We have seen that this question is important during early adulthood. Career direction is a primary concern for both men and women. Yet it falls within a broader consideration—that of sorting out and determining overall life direction. Two related faith responses were prominent during the late teens and early twenties. They were defining what one believes and discovering God's will for one's life. This latter response was very much related to vocational choice.

By the late twenties most individuals were engaged in a career; however, for many the future still seemed unsettled. If a woman was married and had become a mother, she usually found her time increasingly occupied by domestic responsibilities. Judy Potter, for example, wondered after she had become a parent how she would leave her mark on the world. Yet she also developed a new awareness that guiding children was important. As a result, she became more active in church programs for children. At the same time, Judy's faith became less intellectual and more personal. The same was true for many others also.

For those individuals who had been working in the same job for a number of years, somewhere around age thirty became a time to evaluate earlier decisions and to begin to make modifications, if desired, for the future.

Ralph Banks, who changed careers when he was thirty, discovered it to be a time of increased personal crisis followed by increased trust in God. Roberta Spire was still trying to orient her life and restructure her inner self. She, too, found it to be a time of increased trust. Robert Warner felt less emotional about faith, but he was also learning to accept life and God without having to have every question answered. He, also wrestled with a possible career change.

By the mid- to late thirties a number of individuals began to run into dead end roads, or they encountered problems related to career or finances. These individuals came to a point in their lives where they admitted to themselves that they needed help from someone else. This admission led to a new dependency upon God. In the midst of these circumstances, the drive to succeed or to become somebody became reevaluated in light of one's relationship to God and family needs. Frequently, there was a new emphasis upon doing what God wanted, upon serving, and upon rearranging priorities; career ambitions grew less important or became significantly modified. David Spencer, who had no clearly defined career goals, found his mid-thirties to be a time of stagnation, both in terms of his spiritual life as well as his career. As a custodian and maintenance man, he felt like he was going through a daily routine.

Career concerns continued to be present during the forties. For several individuals, faith in God prompted either changing careers or thoughts about changing careers during this time. One individual decided to become a minister. Bill Fitzhugh, a doctor, also felt that God was leading him to change careers, but he was uncertain about any specifics. Having just become a Christian, he felt that he should give back after having received so much. One man, who felt trapped in his job, believed his faith helped him to endure. Another, who had endured a personal crisis, believed that faith in God provided stability for him, even though he had felt alienated from God at the time.

When Albert Spencer was fifty-eight he possessed a new enthusiasm for his career as a minister. He believed that God had granted him a new vision for ministry. In contrast, Raymond Freemont, who was fifty-seven and also a minister, realized that some of his career goals would never be accomplished. Feeling that his good years were behind him, he just did not want to die on the vine. Bert Good retired when he was sixty-three in order to devote more of his time to serving God.

Later adulthood also reflected a variety of responses to career and faith. Most individuals retire during this period. For the most part, career concerns decline in importance and for many, simply become past memories. However, that is not to say that financial concerns cease or that individuals stop working. John Leighland felt that he worked harder after retirement focusing on leisure activities than he had earlier in life. Max Springer recalled that most of his life had been consumed by earning a living. During his retirement years he felt he had more time to give to God. Others shared this sentiment.

In summary, many individuals faced common concerns during their twenties, but from the mid-thirties on, a broader range of career concerns and faith responses emerged. During the twenties, the single largest issue was defining vocational choice. That was very much related to finding God's will and sorting out what one believed to be true about faith and life. Later, issues of trust took on more prominence. Faith in God had to be renegotiated in response to important life changes. Naturally these changes and their associated issues differed from one individual to the next. Such diversity resulted in a variety of faith responses, but with a major focus upon prayer, trust, and reliance upon the power of God. For many, it was during the mid- to late thirties that a recognition developed that what was believed to have been trust in God was actually faith in one's self. The pressure to succeed often drove men to place high emphasis upon their careers, frequently at the expense of their families. When problems erupted, some experienced a reorientation of priorities resulting in less trust in one's self and more dependence upon God.

Trust continued to be a significant faith response related to career throughout the remainder of life. For some, such trust was related to career changes. Others, who felt trapped in a career or who went through a personal crisis, believed that God had sustained them and that their faith provided stability in the midst of turmoil. For many, old age brought new opportunities to serve God since retirement brought more free time.

For the Christian, work should be more than a means to earn money or to survive. It should be viewed as service to God and neighbor. Once an individual has a personal encounter with Jesus Christ, God's calling must take preeminence in life. Being a worker, a parent, a spouse, or a citizen is no longer enough; God's grace lays claim upon each of us.[2] From this personal encounter faith is born, and that faith is expressed by surrendering one's life to the call of God. Work, then, must be viewed in the context of spiritual regeneration. The Christian is not simply to labor, but to labor unto Christ.

From this perspective, work should be seen as a contribution to the welfare of the community and of humanity in general. "Work" is a vehicle for expressing the essence of the new commandment to love one another (2 John 5). The dignity of work is unrelated to *what* is done, but to *why* it is done.[3] Faith is to be expressed through work—work that glorifies God and which serves the human community.

Nevertheless, work should not consume our lives. God has commanded that we are to rest on the Sabbath. When work becomes the number one priority in a person's life, faith in God easily becomes replaced by faith in one's self. Work is to be a service, but even when service becomes all-important—controlling time, energies, and resources—it no longer edifies but destroys. For some, work becomes a god capable of granting great power, wealth, and prestige. Such an obsession can grip the heart; it can initiate a relentless quest that only leads to self-destruction. Tragically, others are destroyed along the way.

God created Man to enjoy life, not to be consumed by it. The command to subdue creation came before the curse of toil. Work is a part of God's divine plan. Sin and death have distorted the nature of work, but for the Christian, the true purpose of work should be reflected in our service to God and neighbor. Christians also toil but we are to express an enlightened understanding of work as service to God. It is not what is done that makes work a spiritual enterprise, but why it is done. Work responds to the call of God and reflects faith that comes from a personal encounter with Jesus Christ. Jesus said,

> Come to me, all you who are weary and burdened, and I will give you rest. Take my yoke upon you and learn from me, for I am gentle and humble in heart, and you will find rest for your souls. For my yoke is easy and my burden is light. (Matt. 11:28–30)

Faith and Family Life

The family plays a central role in the development of most people. One way to understand how a family functions is to consider it as a network of relationships. First there is the relationship between the husband and the wife. Their interaction, shared goals, and mutual commitments have a profound influence on the family. The loss of one's spouse, through either death or divorce, radically alters the nature of family life. Second, there is the relationship between the parents and the children. This relationship is influenced by the gender and by the ages of both the child and parent. Younger children, for example, are more dependent upon their parents than are older children. Furthermore, the nature of that dependency changes with age. Third, if there is more than one child, there is the relationship between siblings. And finally, familial relationships may exist with other relatives such as grandparents, aunts, uncles, and cousins. The nature and extent of these relationships varies from one family to another. However, all of these relationships affect the development and expression of faith.

First, family members shape each other's lives both directly and indirectly. They affect each other directly through personal interaction which has been conditioned by communication patterns, the expressions of love and emotion, and the family power-structures. Second, family members also influence one another indirectly, because what happens to one member affects the whole network of relationships.

Stages of Family Life

As the family develops and changes over time, the nature of family interaction is modified. Families experience stages in much the same way that individuals go through developmental periods. Basically, the stages of family life can be divided as follows:[4]

1. *Establishment.* This stage is characterized by courtship, marriage, and the establishment of marital roles and expectations.

2. *New parents.* The main issues here include pregnancy, birth, care of infant, financial loss if the wife stops working, and new roles and responsibilities as parents. Both parents may feel anxiety, exhaustion and occasional discouragement.

3. *Family with preschool children.* Child development and issues related to autonomy and discipline become important concerns in this stage.

4. *Family with elementary school children.* Education, increased financial expenses, expanding housing needs, establishment of boundaries, and more free time for the wife highlight this period.

5. *Family with adolescent children.* Issues related to an expanding budget, moral behavior, freedom, independence, sexuality, parental authority, education, and career choices make this a potentially turbulent time for both parents and children.

6. *Launching young adults.* The redefinition of roles and relationships between parents and children becomes the central theme of this stage.

7. *No children at home.* Husband-wife relationship, personal careers, and redistribution of power and money are significant issues.

8. *Grandparenthood.* Issues depend upon the style of grandparenting, the location of children and the frequency of contact.

9. *Retirement.* Main issues include finances, leisure time, self-worth, husband-wife interaction and health concerns.

10. *Aging and death.* Health, housing, transportation, bereavement, personal reflection, loneliness, and emotional support are critical concerns during this stage.

The first five stages represent expanding phases of family life. During this period the family grows initially in numbers of members and then continually in terms of needed space, income, goods and services. Commencing with stage six, the family begins to contract as children start to leave home. Expenses begin to decline leaving more discretionary funds. Often, by this time, women have reentered the labor force if they were not already working.

Most families maintain consistency and stability as they go through transition periods. Established patterns of behavior do not disappear overnight, yet over time changes do occur. For example, when a baby is born or when the last child leaves home, major changes are likely to follow affecting family roles, interaction, and responsibilities. Adjustment to these changes normally takes time. During the transition period, conflict is likely to develop as new expectations are formed and new roles are improvised. After a while though, new patterns of behavior are established and once they are settled into, things seem back to "normal." Yet the family is no longer the same as it used to be. The structures of power, communication, and affection may have all been modified. Not only has the family changed, but individual members have changed as well. It is normal to approach transitions with some degree of apprehension. As Joan Aldous has noted, "Regardless of how much prior expectation, preparation, and role rehersal there may have been for these and similar critical changes, the individuals and groups affected encounter the experience with some uncertainty."[5] One of the rewarding aspects of family life, though, is that members can support one another during times of increased stress or turbulence. Of course, the degree and nature of family support is tied to other factors descriptive of the quality of family life. One of these factors is faith.

In reality, the family is a constantly changing entity as individual members move in and out of family roles. The family is also influenced by outside systems. The economy, vocation, education, religious beliefs, law, health care, the military, and other institutional forces all make an impact on family life. All of these factors plus the developmental nature of family interaction influence the nurture and expression of faith.

Several issues related to faith and family life surfaced in early adulthood during the individual interviews. After leaving home, those young adults who had grown up in the church found it necessary to renegotiate their own faith in God. As Sarah Dobbins put it: "There is a stage in life where you stop leaning on your parent's faith and develop your own." Larry Griffin commented, "I realized I was on my own. . . . I had to decide if there was anything to Christianity."

Tony Sampson's family life affected him quite differently. His parents' divorce, followed by the death of his father, launched Tony into a turbulent and traumatic transition into adulthood. Tony's faith in God was a response to not only a lack of direction, but also to a need for love, security, and meaning to life.

Faith in God should and does influence the nature of the marital commitment. Larry Griffin had fallen in love with a non-Christian woman. Though it was painful for him, he made the decision to sever the relationship unless she, too, became a Christian. Linda McDonald married a non-Christian which sabotaged her relationship with God. Later, after her divorce, faith in God helped her to pull her life back together and to regain a sense of purpose and direction. That does not mean that every person who marries a non-Christian will end up divorced, uphappy, or apostate. Yet it must be forcefully stated that such marriages are likely to undercut faith in God and should never be encouraged or promoted within the church. When they do occur, however, it is the responsibility of the Christian spouse to provide spiritual direction for the children and to be loving and faithful to one's spouse. The church must also provide a supportive environment to nuture the spiritual growth of that family.

Just because two people are Christians, though, does not guarantee a successful or happy marriage. Phil and Sally Carpenter, who were married as teen-agers, nearly saw their marriage destroyed for lack of personal maturity and clear direction concerning family and career goals. They were not socially, economically, or psychologically ready for marriage. In the end faith in God held their marriage together.

A number of marriages were saved because of faith in God. Dwain Saunders was still a Christian because of his wife Stacey's faithfulness to Christ. Samuel Gibbons became a Christian because of his wife. Bill and Barbara Fitzhugh were having severe marital problems until they found Christ. Faith in God can provide stability when families go through a crisis. Fred Linder's faith helped him to remain faithful to his wife as he experienced a personal crisis during middle age. In one instance, however, Amos Clapp claimed that he and his wife were divorced because of incompatible religious beliefs and practices. He was Pentecostal and she was Baptist.

A number of individuals became Christians on the heels of divorce. Richard Larson and Laverne Collins both found Christ in their early forties following marital problems. Ruth Stillman became a Christian after discovering that her husband was having an affair. Ten years later she was divorced; this had a significant impact upon Ruth's faith. She commented, "I don't want to get close to people because I'm afraid of being hurt. That has rubbed off on my faith. The constant awareness of the presence of God is not there. The faith is still there, but I go about my daily business more independent than before."

The loss of one's spouse has a significant influence on the expression of faith. Widowhood can create intense feelings of loneliness. Many widows became more conscious of the abiding presence of God. For some Bible reading also became more important; others, though, felt further away from God.

Also, divorce or widowhood generated a new sense of disorganization. For middle-aged individuals, this led to concerns about career, income, parental responsibilities, and so on. A new concern for discerning the will of God developed. Frequently this was followed by feelings of increased dependency upon God. A number of older single women also looked to God to provide for their needs. They had few other sources for financial help or physical assistance.

Rearing children also affected the development and expression of faith. During the early stages of family life, women tended to be affected more by motherhood than men did by fatherhood. During those years, men were often investing their time and energies into their careers. Women, on the other hand, experienced increased domestic responsibilities and found their lives more taken up with child care and household responsibilities even if they also worked outside the home. Judy Potter commented, "Since the children have come my faith has changed. Earlier in my life I didn't feel the need for faith as much. It was more of an intellectual experience, something that was interesting to discuss. Now I know the Shepherd and not just the psalm."

During their mid-thirties on, men showed an increased interest in family-related issues. Phil Carpenter was concerned about his son who had just turned eleven. Phil remarked, "He's becoming more rebellious." As men deemphasized career goals they tended to focus more on family life. For those individuals who became Christians during their thirties or forties, they became concerned about rearing their children to become Christians. Bill Fitzhugh commented, "I'm concerned about the well-being of our daughter and am praying that she will find the same relationship that we have with God."

When Laverne Collins became a Christian at age forty, she discovered it altered her relationship with her children. She noted, "My children have seen a change in me. There are two who are accepting it and two who don't know what to do with me. My oldest daughter is rebelling against me."

As the children leave home, that can also affect spiritual life. When Barbara Fitzhugh's daughter left to go to college, it had a dramatic effect upon her. Barbara commented, "When she left for college it was very traumatic for me. I was very sad. We were both scared to death to send her to college. I started feeling like my daughter didn't need me and that my husband didn't need me. Those were very down years for me." Ultimately, that experience led Barbara to become a Christian.

Becoming a Christian later in life affected Thelma Watson's relationship with her grandchildren. At age sixty-three, she had only been a Christian four years. She noted, "My personality has changed. I was going through a thing with my granddaughters. They were a little wild and it was making me turn against them. But after I was saved I looked at them with more compassion. Rather than criticize them like I had been doing, I looked beyond their faults."

Family life affects spiritual growth. The fluid and dynamic nature of family development has an effect upon the nurture and expression of faith. Important transitions like becoming parents, children leaving home, divorce, or loss of a spouse affect family interaction. This affects other areas of life including one's relationship with God. Children growing up in a Christian home must eventually cultivate belief in God apart from their parent's faith. Parents, on the other hand, who become Christians later in life, will feel a new urgency to shape the faith development of their children. Depending upon the age of the children and the attitude of the parent and child, this can lead either to conflict or to greater understanding and acceptance. The dissolution of the family during old age often leads to a heightened awareness of God's presence and an anticipation of meeting loved ones in heaven. As Iva Robinson commented to her husband on her death bed, "Make sure I meet the kids in heaven."

Just as the life structure of the individual changes as it goes through transition periods, so too, family structures also change over time. These changes require a variety of strategies and responses in order to provide an adequate and supportive framework for healthy family life. Faith in God provides a foundation for family unity and cohesiveness, although one family member may experience and express faith quite differently

from another. Needs and perceptions may vary greatly from one member
to another. These factors must be taken into account in nurturing both
faith and family life.

Faith and Health

Those with health problems have always been attracted to Jesus. In the
Gospel of Mark we are told that the whole town came to Jesus, and that
Jesus healed many who had various diseases (1:33f.). Jesus' healing
ministry lured crowds for two reasons. First, those who were sick saw
in Jesus a source of hope. They believed he could make them well.
Second, the multitudes thrived on the miraculous. Human curiosity draws
people to the supernatural, to the bizarre, to the miraculous. Such
curiosity, though, is never satisfied. One sign or miracle only leaves
the crowd demanding another.

While Jesus had compassion on the sick, he had no sympathy for
miracle-seekers. He refused to perform miracles to gratify the doubters
or the sign-seekers. Yet he pointed to his miracles as an indication that
he was the Messiah. The scriptures tell us that many people saw the
miraculous signs he was doing and believed in him. Yet Jesus did not
entrust himself to these individuals because "he knew all men" (John
2:24). True faith sees beyond the miracle to the person of Jesus himself.

Jesus' healing of the sick is more than divine medical care; rather,
it points to the new age, to the Kingdom of God. The miracles are signs
of that which is to come. The healing miracles demonstrate that this
Kingdom is more than just a subjective reality. It is not wish fulfillment.
Such healing reflects an assault on the powers of darkness.

Jesus oriented his ministry to the poor, the blind, the lame, and the
deaf—to those without power and status—and their lives became
transformed by faith in the Son of God. When John the Baptist began
to have second thoughts whether or not Jesus was the Messiah, Jesus
told John's disciples, "The blind receive sight, the lame walk, those who
have leprosy are cured, the deaf hear, the dead are raised, and the good
news is preached to the poor" (Matt. 11:5). Those were the signs that
God's Kingdom was imminent. Those without hope, who were scorned
as sinners and social outcasts, became the recipients of God's grace. Jesus
Christ is the bearer of salvation.

Such actions prompted reprisals and rebukes from the religious
establishment; they still do today. The spirituality of the Pharisees,

Sadducees and other religious leaders caused them to be blind to the significance of Jesus' healings. They took Jesus to task for healing on the Sabbath. They claimed he performed miracles by the power of the devil. They charged him with blasphemy. Healing stirs controversy. It did then and it still does now. We must ask, what place does healing have in the church today? And furthermore, what is the relationship between faith and healing?

Jesus sent out his disciples to heal the sick. Such ministry continued after the resurrection. Healing stories are present in the Book of Acts: the lame walked (3:6f.); the dead were raised (9:37f.); and the sick were made well (5:16). Prayer for the sick became part of the Christian tradition. James wrote: "Is any one of you sick? He should call the elders of the church to pray over him and anoint him with oil in the name of the Lord. And the prayer offered in faith will make the sick person well; the Lord will raise him up" (James 5:14f.).

Prayer for the sick is an integral aspect of faith and practice. Such prayer points to another dimension of reality by reminding us constantly that salvation has dawned. Death and sin have been conquered. But is such prayer simply a form or a ritual? Is it no more than a way of comforting the afflicted? Can one truly expect God to raise someone from the dead? What does prayer for the sick imply and what should the Christian expect from such prayer?

As the most intimate form of communication prayer reveals our hearts. Before we speak, God knows our needs and inner-most thoughts. In the act of prayer nothing new is revealed to God, but through prayer, we are changed. Prayer awakens the Christian to the reality of God's Kingdom. Prayer brings into focus the nature of our spiritual conflict. We are reminded of the disparity between our heavenly citizenship and our earthly existence.

Jesus goes to the wilderness to pray. He prays alone. There he must come to grips with the purpose of his mission. In the desert Satan confronts him. Later the crowds acclaim him and would make him a ruler. They believe in him because of his miracles. Yet in prayer the comprehensive nature of sin and death stand out in bold relief against a holy God. Prayer strips away the glamour and tinsel of earthly achievement. Human success fades in importance when seen in the light of humanity's death-infested existence. Yet at the same time, the holiness and power of God lift us to new heights of commitment and strength.

Seen in this light, prayer for the sick is an embodiment of the prayer,

"Thy Kingdom come." Prayer for the sick is more than spiritual comfort or the hope for physical healing although it includes both of these aspects. It is a continual reminder that in Christ we have life. Apart from him there is nothing but death. Such prayer is made with confidence that God is the Creator and Sustainer of life. The primary focus of prayer for the sick is life. We trust God for healing, but one can be healed and yet forfeit existence. The issue is not simply physical well-being, but *existence*—more precisely, *eternal life.*

No such thing as divine health exists this side of heaven. Paul states that we have the "firstfruits" of the Spirit, not the "fullfruits." We, like the rest of creation, groan inwardly as we wait eagerly for the redemption of our bodies (Rom. 8:23). Though outwardly we are wasting away, yet inwardly we are being renewed day by day (2 Cor. 4:16). The Holy Spirit has been given to us as a deposit guaranteeing what is to come (2 Cor. 5:5). What is to come? The new age and all of its benefits including a new body. In part, John describes it as follows:

> And I heard a loud voice from the throne saying, "Now the dwelling of God is with men, and he will live with them. They will be his people, and God himself will be with them and be their God. He will wipe every tear from their eyes. There will be no more death or mourning or crying or pain, for the old order of things has passed away." (Rev. 21:3-4)

Notice, when this occurs, the old order has passed away. This does not occur until death is destroyed (1 Cor. 15:25-28). Until then, Christians still die, but the "sting" of death has been removed (1 Cor. 15:55). In Christ we experience eternal life regardless of physical health.

This is not to say that healing does not occur in this age. On various occasions the signs of the age to come—i.e. healing—are manifest. Jesus and his disciples healed the sick, and testimonies of healing have always circulated in the church. We are to pray and trust God for healing, but we must also face reality. Not everyone who is prayed for is healed. Devout, faithful, committed Christians die of illness, even though many have prayed on their behalf. Does that mean that there was a lack of faith or that sin was present prohibiting God from healing?

Some Christians would argue that something must have been wrong otherwise healing would have taken place. These individuals, while they have good intentions, often leave a trail of sorrow and guilt in the lives of their innocent victims.

When I was a college student, a dear personal friend of mine died of cancer. He was a leader in our church and a man of unwavering Christian commitment. His entire family reflected his own dedication and zeal to serve God. He and his family exemplified Christian charity and service.

By the time he saw a doctor, the cancer had progressed too far to be successfully treated. Although our church prayed for him, his condition steadily worsened until he was eventually confined to a bed at home.

Several days before he died, I visited him. He told me, "Jim, I've prayed that God will heal me, but there's one thing I know. I could never have learned to trust him like I have until this came upon me. I've learned things the past few months about myself and about him that I could have never of learned otherwise. I'm ready to meet him. I'm like Paul, 'to live is Christ, to die is gain.' "

Faith is a relationship with Jesus Christ that transcends physical circumstances. Some people try to turn faith into a quantity. It's like putting gas in your car. Your tank can be full, half-full, or empty. If you have a little faith you can trust God to find you a parking place. If you have more faith, maybe he will give you an expensive car to park in it. And so on. Faith understood in this way misses the entire thrust of the New Testament. Faith is not a quantity, it is a relationship. It is not simply characterized by what one believes, but how one lives. Faith is not measured by the number of prayers which are answered, but by the nature of one's service and heart. Faith transcends circumstances and embraces the Eternal. Faith in Jesus Christ brings life, even in the clutches of death. My friend may have died of cancer, yet he lives in Christ. That is the bottom line of faith.

As we examine the impact of health on the development and expression of faith in the lives of those interviewed, we discover that it played a major role regardless of age. Health problems or accidents, experienced either personally or by loved ones, frequently led people to a new dependency on and trust in God. For many, it prompted their own conversion.

Tom Meyer, who was twenty, remembered the impact of a car accident. "My sister was crippled. I was about twelve at the time. That taught me to pray. That gave me something to pray for. I prayed more."

Brian Dunn (age twenty-eight) recalled an important event that occurred when he was fourteen.

"I broke my arm and when the doctor examined it, he discovered a tumor. There was concern that it was malignant. The doctor thought my arm would have to be amputated, but he waited. The tumor began to shrink. It's virtually gone now. At the time it happened, I had no idea of the seriousness of it. It became more important to me later in life. I didn't find out until several years later how serious it could have been. We went to the Christian Missionary Alliance Church and healing wasn't greatly emphasized. Now I look back on it and realize that God has worked on my physical life.''

The healing of Brian's tumor bolstered his faith as a young adult. Health concerns also had a major impact on Robert Warner's conversion and maturing as a Christian. Bob suffered a serious injury while playing football at school when he was fourteen. He was hospitalized for nine weeks and had to have a kidney removed. At that time he was not a Christian.

''I remember the kid next to me had leukemia. He died several months later. I wondered why he died and I lived. I was the first-string quarterback on the school team. After the accident I couldn't play anymore. I realized that people liked the quarterback rather than 'Bob'; it left me bitter.

Due to that experience and a concerned teacher, Bob later became a Christian. While in college Bob's faith was tested when a friend died of cancer. Through that experience he realized that there were some open-ended questions in life. Bob described that as the end of his childhood faith. There was less enthusiasm but more stability.

George Hayes became a Christian at age fifty-two as the result of health problems. He was seventy-two years of age at the time I interviewed him. His wife was sixty-nine.

Mr. Hayes: ''Twenty years ago I had gall bladder surgery. I really got sick and I was mad at my brother-in-law. We were having some real problems. My blood pressure was also high and I was having some trouble with my heart beating too fast. I was so weak that I couldn't even dress myself.

''While I was in the hospital several ladies from the church came and prayed for me. They asked me if I was ready to put it all on the altar. I didn't know much about God, but I told them I would and I did. I gave my life to God. I stopped drinking and smoking. There was a radical change in my life.''

Mrs. Hayes: ''That was a trying time for me. His mother and my mother were in a nursing home at the same time. I had to take care of all three of them. His mother died in April that year and my mother died in August. It was a hard time.

''I didn't question God, but I would get depressed. There were days

I didn't feel I could go on. Somehow I got the strength to go on for another day. I have stronger faith now. I understand better and feel God is closer.''

Mr. Hayes: ''Things are different now. Now we visit the sick. I didn't do that before. I pray out loud publicly at church. Since I've retired we visit shut-ins. We also have a Bible study at our house on Tuesday nights.''

As the result of health and family problems, Mr. Hayes experienced a major change in his life at about age fifty. The changes in his life affect Mrs. Hayes.

The health concerns of one's spouse often have a serious impact on faith in God. Steve Learner found his faith tested shortly after he became a Christian at the age of twenty-five.

''My wife and I lost a baby at birth right after I became a Christian. My wife almost died too. I had a lot of questions. At first, I felt like leaving God. Then about three years later my wife had brain surgery. It put a lot of stress on me and the kids. There was a good chance she would come out paralyzed on one side. I found myself questioning God again. There was a nurse in the hospital that was a Christian. She shared with both of us. After the surgery, I found that my faith had grown. I was more mature. Now we're able to minister to other people going through the same kind of trauma.''

Steve's wife made it through the surgery successfully. There are other occasions, however, when things do not go right. The death of loved ones, especially children, raises many questions for people about faith and the will of God. For some it draws them closer to God as they lean on him for support. For others it causes extended trauma and grief. Rick Singer found it as a time to grow closer to God.

When my son was killed in 1975, that was the first time my faith was really tested. Before that everything was just theory. That was the test. That let me know God was for real. When you're in the valley and God brings you out of it emotionally, mentally and spiritually, you realize that God is able to sustain you in times of need.''

Alice Strong (age seventy-four) also recalled how God sustained her family through a similar difficulty.

''The most difficult time I can recall is when my granddaughter died. She was always a sick child and died when she was four years old. It was the middle of winter and there was six feet of snow on the ground. My daughter said, 'How can we bury Corie in six feet of snow?' Suddenly she raised her hands and began to praise God. We all prayed and then she said, 'I'm all right.' We had the funeral the next day. Somehow God took the burden upon himself.''

Rita Lindell's child died of leukemia. Rita believed up until the last moment that God would intervene. An earlier healing in her own life gave her confidence that God would heal her son. When he was not healed it was a blow to her faith.

"My faith has had its ups and downs. I used to have an incurable disease called *diabetes insipidus*. It's when you have trouble with your pituitary gland. I was having to take shots every other day. One night at church I heard the Lord speak to me, ''You're healed, but don't go to the doctor for one year.'' I told my husband that I was stopping the shots and I did. God completely healed me. When I went to the doctor he gave me a clean bill of health. I had been taking those shots for seven years!

"I guess that's why when our son got sick I believed the Lord could heal him. He got leukemia and the doctor only gave him six months to live. I just knew the Lord would heal him and I believed it up until the last. Chris would get pretty bad and I would start to worry and I would think, He's not dead yet. The Lord will heal him. I just believed that clear up until he died.

"I felt guilty after he died, but I also had a sense of peace. At first I thought I didn't have enough faith or had done something wrong. Then I thought maybe there was something wrong with Chris. I just had to work through it. I feel I've done that. I feel like I've always had faith but it's been up and down. At first after he died it was hard. I've always had peace cause I know he's with the Lord, but I still miss him.''

It took Rita Lindell several months to work through her feelings of guilt. She was so convinced that God would heal her son, that when it did not happen, she concluded either that she did not have enough faith or that she or her son had committed some sin that had prevented God from doing a miracle.

Throughout the interviews, and especially from those fifty and over, health concerns had a major impact on faith development. Health problems or accidents normally led people to develop a greater dependency upon God. It made them reflect more upon their own mortality. It also caused people to raise questions about God's will. For some it led to their conversion; for others, health problems raised feelings of guilt, anger, and caused belief in God to waver.

Before going to the next section, there is a final story that serves to highlight theological issues related to healing and faith. Paul Hiebert, Professor of Anthropology and South Asian Studies at Fuller School of World Missions recounted the following event which took place while he served as a missionary in India.[6] A prayer meeting was held on behalf of a child who later died. Paul Hiebert felt defeated. He asked himself, Who was I to be a missionary if I could not pray for healing and receive a positive answer? Shortly after that one of the village men contacted him with a sense of triumph and joy. Paul asked, "How can you be so happy after the child died?"

The man responded, "The village would have acknowledged the power of our God had he healed the child, but they knew in the end she would have to die. When they saw in the funeral our hope of resurrection and reunion in heaven, they saw an even greater victory, over death itself, and they have begun to ask about the Christian way."

While every human being expresses genuine concerns about health, the ultimate issue is not healing but life. Like my friend, those with faith in Christ are able to say, "To live is Christ, to die is gain."

Faith and Death

Nothing draws a person closer to God any more than death or the belief that one is going to die. When faced with no earthly future, eternal concerns become more urgent. As the convict leaves his cell on death row, there is the ever-present clergyman reciting the Lord's Prayer. Eternity now hangs in the balance. Death brings a sense of ultimacy.

The nearness of death does have an impact on the expression of faith. While concerns related to mortality begin to surface with the loss of parents or other loved ones during middle age, the personal awareness of the reality of death intensifies as one enters later adulthood. As indicated earlier, studies have revealed that the fear of death tends to decline with age. How one responds to death is related to how satisfactorily certain spiritual, psychological, and social tasks have been addressed. For example, a person may feel prepared to meet God, but can be weighed down by concerns about family members he or she will leave behind. Issues related to insurance, wills, financial arrangements, and "leave-taking" with individual family members, friends, and perhaps even enemies can be very important to the social and psychological tasks of dying. Older adults may benefit by retelling their life story and reflecting on important memories. This provides an opportunity to summarize their life and to psychologically tie things together. Often we are concerned about helping people to live. Perhaps we are unaware that we must also help people to die. That means more than spiritual preparation. So often we assume that if a person is a Christian, then that is all that matters as they approach death. However, Christians need support in dying just like they need support in living.

Theologically, there is another dimension to death that must be recognized and addressed. Death is more than biological termination and it takes on many forms. A person can be physically alive, but dead socially, psychologically, or spiritually. Death has infected all of creation and nothing has been left untainted.

Death is more than an individual reality. It is also embedded in every structure and institution, regardless of purpose or goals. While death is symbolized by weapons of military destruction, it is no less a part of government, business, industry, medicine, education, and every other existing institution. The pervasive and comprehensive nature of death emanates from the fallen state of creation.

These institutions all offer hope for a better life. But from a biblical perspective, all that they can ultimately offer is of no eternal value. The end will always be the same—death. Yet death can be presented in a way that makes it palatable to Man. In a more overt form it may come as a military build-up designed to protect national security. More subtly, it is reflected in the pursuit of the "American Dream." Ultimately, life cannot be secured by nuclear weapons nor found through material gain. The end of both is the same—death. Apart from Christ there is no escaping death.

Once the inevitability of death is recognized—in any of its forms—individuals are more likely to respond to the gospel. Jesus said, "The thief comes only to steal and kill and destroy; I have come that they may have life, and have it to the full" (John 10:10). When death comes into focus, the stark contrast between Satan and Christ becomes clear. One destroys, the other brings life. It is no wonder that those who confront death face-to-face discover a new attraction to Jesus. The presence of death gives new power to Jesus' statement: "I am the resurrection and the life. He who believes in me will live, even though he dies" (John 11:25). The full impact of these words can never be fully appreciated until one encounters death at a personal level.

Our study indicated that for most people, physical death did not surface as a developmental issue until middle age. A few individuals experienced accidents or health problems during early adulthood that brought the inevitability of death into more clear focus for a time. For at least one individual, that prompted his conversion.

The awareness of death during middle age tended to make people aware of time limitations. Most individuals still had goals in life. For some, that awareness created a new sense of urgency to accomplish certain tasks. Bill Fitzhugh commented, "I have a greater sense of urgency now. I don't have time to waste." Yet for others, it made them feel the need to slow down and perhaps work less and play more. Richard Larson remarked, "You've got to stop and smell the roses. . . . You only go around once. If you don't slow down you'll wind up going to the grave still looking for it."

Those in later adulthood also developed a heightened awareness of death. But for them it was something more personal and less abstract than what those experienced in middle age. Those in their forties came to the realization that life is finite and that time is limited. Those in later adulthood, though, recognized that death was near—"I will die soon." More attention was given to preparing for death. Elaine Whitt, who was sixty-seven, commented, "I think about my future and am trying to prepare for my own death. I want to be ready, to know that I'll be with Christ." Mildred Albright, seventy-two, said, "You know you don't have much time left. You've got to get close to God now or you don't get another chance later."

For some in later adulthood, the nearness of death brought new feelings of assurance and an increased awareness of God's abiding presence. There was less focus on materialism and more concern about spiritual matters. In middle adulthood, the awareness of death prompted increased trust in God, but death was still a distant reality. It helped to intensify goals and strip away illusions. Life goals became viewed more realistically. In any form, death reminds us of the preciousness of life.

Faith and Life Transitions

All transitions share one thing in common—in some way a person's life is changed. The more stable a person's life, the better prepared they are to cope with change. We have seen that faith serves as a stablizing force in the lives of many people as they experience major transitions throughout life. The quality of a person's faith, though, is also related to important factors such as congregational support, family life, health, the Bible, prayer, and person commitment. Faith is not an abstract quality separated from the rest of life. It is directly related to life events. Life transitions play a prominent role in the development and expression of faith.

As we mentioned earlier, there are two main types of transitions. The first is an extended period of time lasting three to five years that serves as a bridge between two stable periods of adult development. For example, the period from about thirty-eight to forty-three serves as a transition period from early to middle adulthood. During such periods a person may experience fundamental changes in his or her life structure.

Individuals also experience transition events. These may include such events as leaving home, getting married, becoming parents, moving, menopause, retirement, or accidents. Frequently these events serve as milestones which act as reference points as we reflect on our lives. Normally, they entail some adjustments or adaptations in lifestyle.

During transition periods, decisions made earlier in life are often reviewed and evaluated. Often this results in modifications in how a person structures his or her life. These changes are sometimes voluntary, but at other times they are beyond the control of the individual. They can lead to feelings of greater security and happiness or to a greater sense of urgency and concern about life direction. On occasion, they may lead to a radical break with the past. They may also serve as a platform for a smooth transition into the next period of life. Levinson suggests that such transitions occur throughout adulthood at about ten year intervals commencing around age eighteen.

Faith plays a major role during these transition periods. Many individuals become Christians during these times as they wrestle with important concerns and life direction. Others, who are already Christians, frequently find these periods to be times of personal growth and maturity. The way that one expresses faith may change related to new developmental issues and tasks. On some occasions it may also lead to questions or doubts. This was more likely to occur during times of personal loss or crisis related to an accident, divorce, death, loss of a job or a similar type of event. On other occasions, however, these same events caused people to draw closer to God.

Transition periods or events also prompted reflection about discerning the will of God. While this was a very common experience for young adults after they left home, it also recurred later in life as well. After her divorce, for example, Linda McDonald, thirty-five, remarked, "I don't have the same 'I know, that I know' as I did as a kid. I'm not sure if I should rest in the Lord or if I should go out there and find out what I should be."

When Pam Wilburn was thirty-seven, her husband died of cancer. Pam commented, "I have to reenter the world and make a living. I'm also trying to raise a teenage son. I'm trying to find God's will."

Ralph Bennett, a minister, had just completed building a new church facility. He felt like he was at a crossroads in his life. Ralph said, "I want to know that I'm at the place where God wants me to be."

Discerning God's will is an important issue throughout life. In early adulthood it plays a prominent role related to major choices concerning life direction. Later in life it tends to resurface during transition periods and after significant events which lead to disorganization or cause concerns about the future.

In summary, life transitions play a critical role in the formation, development, and expression of faith throughout the adult life cycle. They provide opportunities for ministry, both to the believer and the nonbeliever. They may lead to a person's conversion or to personal growth. In some instances they lead to doubts and cause people to question God.

We have seen that the development and expression of faith interacts with important issues and tasks throughout the adult life cycle. Many of these issues are related to career, family life, health, and death. Furthermore, each of these developmental areas is interrelated and affects the development and modification of a person's life structure. Life transitions also serve as important points or periods when faith development occurs.

One question remains: Is there some normative dimension to faith? That is, what is mature faith? When, if ever, is it experienced? Does it come only later in life? Is it experienced by only a few? How is it to be recognized?

Faith and the Kingdom of God

James Fowler believes that there is a stage of faith that comes the closest to embodying the Kingdom of God. Those who represent this stage are not perfect, yet they manifest a special grace that transcends normal standards of righteousness. Yet, he believes that there are only a few who actually experience what he calls "universalizing faith."[7]

Certainly, we have all encountered certain "faithful" men and women who reflect the life of Christ in a special way. Then there are always a multitude of others who hang around the fringe. They are attracted to Christ, but they also keep him at a distance. What are the unique characteristics that lead to and reflect Christian maturity?

The scriptures identify different levels of Christian maturity. Paul, for example, instructs his converts to be imitators of his own life in Christ (1 Cor. 4:16f.). The writer of Hebrews differentiates between those who need milk and those able to consume solid food (Heb. 5:13f.). John distinguishes between children, young men and fathers in the faith (1 John 2:12f.).

While there does appear to be different levels of Christian maturity, nowhere are they clearly defined. Obviously, a person's commitment, values and attitude affect Christian growth (Rom. 6:19). Every Christian is encouraged and expected to mature. Furthermore, such growth is a lifelong process.

Every believer has his or her own place within the body of Christ. Not everyone is an apostle, prophet, evangelist, or pastor-teacher. Each person is to serve according to the grace he or she receives from God. In part, Christian maturity is reflected by being a good steward of God's grace. The mature, faithful servant will not necessarily be the most visible or most rewarded member of the congregation. His or her contribution may not even be felt to be important by some. Yet, like the widow who gave all that she had, God may view things quite differently than Man. He alone is the judge of faith.

Mature faith will respond to the same concerns that attracted Jesus. He showed special concern for the poor, imprisoned, blind, and oppressed. He placed no premium upon recognition or acceptance by political or religious leaders. He showed no interest in accumulating possessions or in acquiring power. His concern was for human life. Jesus expressed love and forgiveness. When others would condemn, he spoke words of grace.

At the same time, Jesus made radical demands upon his followers. Those who would follow him must first count the cost. They must take up their cross and follow in his steps. The way of mature faith is costly—it leads to the Cross. It rejects the glitter and tinsel of human recognition, seeking instead the favor of God. Mature faith is most clearly seen in service, which expresses the love of Christ.

Only God can judge such faith. Surely we need more mature Christians. The world is full of poor, blind, imprisoned and oppressed people. It has been said that those who preach to the suffering will never lack for a congregation. We are surrounded by human need. Where are those with faith?

> Whoever wants to become great among you must be your servant, and whoever wants to be first must be slave of all. For even the Son of Man did not come to be served, but to serve, and to give his life a ransom for many. (Mark 10:43–45)

14
Practical Implications

We have arrived at the point where we must ask, 'What is the practical use of all this? What difference does knowledge about faith development make for the life of the church?' There are very important and practical implications related to congregational life and adult development. The developmental nature of faith and adulthood has implications for preaching, education, pastoral care, and evangelism. Nearly every aspect of congregational ministry is touched by concerns related to the findings of this study.

If we are not careful, we can develop a theology of Christian growth which is divorced from the daily issues of life. Somehow, it is believed that if we can pump people full of Bible knowledge that they will automatically grow as Christians. Bible knowledge is critical. It cannot be overemphasized and every Christian needs more of it. Yet cognitive development does not equal Christian growth. Knowledge of the Bible is only effective when it is translated into practical Christian living. That is not an automatic process.

Christian growth is affected by various issues encountered throughout life. Christian faith, however, should affect a person's response to changing life circumstances. Faith is more than belief, it must be translated into practice. It must include the dimensions of trust, hope, obedience, and faithfulness. Faith reflects one's relationship with Jesus Christ. Most importantly, faith is to be expressed through love.

In addition to cognitive development, we must recognize that feelings and emotions have a significant impact on the nature and extent of Christian growth. In addition to intellect and emotions, every person also has a will. It is the combined response of intellect, emotions, and will that affect how faith is expressed.

When we encounter Jesus Christ, we encounter a person, not just an intellect. Jesus is the *Word made flesh*. Jesus cried and he laughed; he felt pain, anger, joy, and sadness. Jesus reflected about his life and mission. He prayed to the Father, "Not as I will, but as you will."

Jesus understands human need. He healed the sick; he embraced children; he went to the poor, the lame, the deaf, to prostitutes and sinners, to tax collectors and Roman soldiers. He is a friend to the friendless, manifesting love, not just facts. Jesus forgives people and points them in a different direction. He brings new life. Jesus summons faith in himself, not in tablets of stone. He and he alone becomes the object of saving faith. And like any relationship with a living person, our relationship with Jesus changes over time. It must change in order to meet the various challenges of different life circumstances.

Christian growth is a lifelong process. That recognition should affect the nature and content of congregational life and ministry. We will begin by examining implications related to preaching.

Preaching

The developmental nature of adulthood shatters the premise that a congregation can be homogeneous. There simply is no such thing. When the pastor stands behind the pulpit on Sunday mornings, he or she is viewing a congregation of unique people facing very different life issues and tasks. One person may have just lost a job. Another is concerned about her elderly mother in the hospital. A young couple have just become parents. A middle-aged woman recently went through a divorce. All of these people may be present physically, but that does not guarantee they are there mentally or emotionally. They have come expecting to encounter Jesus Christ, since he alone can minister to their needs.

On any given Sunday, many needs are present, but most will remain unspoken, hidden in the hearts of men and women, and boys and girls.

By the Holy Spirit, the proclamation of the Word can minister healing and hope to the brokenhearted and discouraged. It can bring light into darkness. Sin can be unmasked, forgiveness can be embraced, and new life can begin.

But this can only occur to the extent that the spoken word addresses the needs of those who hear. We have seen that Christian growth is very much related to developmental issues and tasks associated with various periods of the life cycle. The preacher needs to be informed concerning these issues and to use appropriate illustrations related to career, family life, health concerns, and other vital issues which are of critical concern to those who are present. The sermon must move beyond the cognitive dimension to encounter the hearts of those who hear. It must enter behind the closed doors of a person's life and confront issues related to life and death.

I am not suggesting that congregational needs should be the guiding light determining what is preached. The scriptures should give definition to preaching. But as that text is proclaimed, it must expose and enlighten those who hear it to the grace of God or no real communication has occurred. It must be applied to the life context of those who hear.

An understanding of faith and adult development can help the pastor to speak to specific issues and concerns facing congregational members. That does not mean that every sermon must revolve around developmental themes. However, they should be appropriately integrated and used to speak to important life issues on a regular basis. Relevant preaching cannot avoid the issues of life.

One practical application might be to develop a series of biographical sermons focusing on the life of David or Moses. This would provide an excellent opportunity to address developmental issues from a theological perspective.

Education

The fact that personal, family and congregational needs change over time has important implications for Christian education. It is possible for church leaders and teachers to invest time, resources, and energy into programs and classes which are not in touch with people's needs. If our goal is to equip Christians for service and to strengthen faith, then we must focus on relevant and important life issues and needs. Otherwise, we may end up answering questions that no one is asking.

The key to successful adult education is to develop learning activities in which the setting, content, and learning process are supportive of learner needs and which are relevant to a participant's interest and goals. These events should be planned and conducted utilizing knowledge related to adult development.

Two initial questions must be asked: What needs to be learned? What will be the content of our educational activities?

At the outset it is important to recognize that formal education is not the measuring rod of Christian growth. It is obvious that the early church did not engage in all of the educational "techniques" of goal setting, curriculum design, need assessments, or evaluation processes associated with education today. Yet, the early church did engage in formal educational activities based upon rabbinic traditions, and they recognized the need for instruction in the synagogues and at home. It became important very early in the life of the church to provide instruction concerning the historical ministry of Jesus and the significance of his death and resurrection. Problems created by heretics forced the need for doctrinal instruction and clarification. New believers were educated about conduct with respect to family life, work, and social involvement. It is clear that Christians needed then, and need today, a body of knowledge and practical skills related to the following areas: (1) to grow in their relationship to and understanding of God; (2) to become equipped for service within the Body of Christ and for ministry to those in need; and, (3) to cope successfully with societal trends and pressures.

What should this body of knowledge include? Obviously, we must begin with the scriptures. Every Christian needs a basic understanding of the truths of salvation. That does not mean, however, that every Christian needs to be able to write an essay exam on covenantal theology or provide a detailed review of the Minor Prophets. Ideally, every Christian will grow in his or her understanding of biblical content. This content is necessary to provide a framework for decision-making consistent with the rule of God. This understanding should be reflected in daily behavior, attitudes, and values. This leads us to a second area of knowledge critical for Christian growth.

Christians, like all human beings, live out their lives in a social context. That is, we interact with other people as part of our daily existence. These people influence us and we also influence them. Normally, this interaction occurs within institutional settings. We are also influenced by these institutions whether they include schools, governmental agencies, corporations, churches, or hospitals.

Christians need to be informed concerning the implications of our faith as it pertains to the different social and institutional environments in which we live out our lives. What does it mean to be a *Christian* husband, wife, consumer, citizen, business person, or student? Our world confronts us as an objective reality. Daily, we must make decisions that affect who we are and who we are becoming. One major task of education within the church is to equip Christians with the knowledge and skills necessary for making informed decisions on important issues of life. Such knowledge and skills must themselves be consistent with biblical truth, Christian commitment, and faith in God.

In light of the above discussion and related to faith development, it is important for adult education programs within the church to offer a diverse variety of subject matter. These events should touch upon significant areas and issues affecting adults in today's world. This might include events related to parent training, marriage, family life, world problems, ethical issues, work, health, and social relationships—in addition to the study of biblical and theological issues.

We must also keep in mind that adults will be at different stages of development in terms of Christian growth, personal maturity, and position within the life cycle. These factors should be taken into consideration when deciding upon content. It must also be recognized that adults engage in educational activities for different reasons. Cyril Houle has identified three main reasons for participation.[1] Some learners are activity-oriented, they love going and doing. This type of learner will be present regardless of the topic. They love social contact. A second type of learner is goal-oriented or problem-oriented. Participation in learning events is tied to a concrete purpose. The goal-oriented learner expects and desires to achieve a specific result. Finally, a third type of adult participant can be described as learning-oriented. This individual enjoys learning for its own sake. These people show interest in a diverse range of subjects.

Adult education classes in the church must take into account all three categories of learners. While every Christian should have the goal of growing and maturing in one's faith, not every believer is dealing with the same issues of life. As we have seen, faith development is very much related to developmental concerns. Subjects like "Parent Training" or "Communication in Marriage" are likely to attract goal-oriented or problem-oriented learners. Knowing and understanding the life context and developmental concerns of the participants is crucial in order to adequately respond to their learning needs. On the other hand, a course on the Protestant Reformation is more likely to attract activity-oriented and learning-oriented participants. Instructors must plan accordingly. Each learner has his or her own personal reasons for involvement and they may not be the same as the instructor's.

Church programs which are responsive to community, family and individual needs are more likely to succeed than those which are not. The popular slogan, "find a need and fill it," is a simple but profound truth with respect to effective ministry. Obviously people have needs. If a local congregation will orient part of its resources, energy, and planning to identify and respond to felt needs within the community and the church, it will obtain valuable information in developing meaningful and strategic programs.

Need assessments should have at least the following three dimensions: *normative, expressed,* and *comparative* analysis. The *normative* level refers to those needs which are always present regardless of the situation. For example, as Christians we always need to grow in our relationship to God and our understanding of the scriptures. In another sense, normative needs are those which are identified and agreed upon by recognized experts in a particular field of study. If you were planning a course on parent training, for example, it would be helpful to discover what experts in this field believe to be the critical issues. This information can be found by doing a literature review of relevant books and articles. Spend some time at the library or at a Christian bookstore reviewing pertinent material.

A second important process in determining needs is simply to ask participants what they sense to be their most significant needs. What are they interested in studying that can be of value and interest to them personally? These are *expressed* needs.

It can also be helpful to examine what other churches are doing in their adult education program. Call up several churches and ask what they are doing in their adult classes. Obtain any written course or program descriptions that they may have. Also, review your church's past programs. Which events were most successful? This process is known as a *comparative* need assessment.

Typically, the best procedure for determining needs is some combination of the above processes. Most importantly, content should reflect both normative and expressed needs. Knowledge related to adult development and Christian growth can help both in the assessment of needs as well as in the planning and implementation of educational programs within the church.

In the most fundamental sense, adult learning within the church arises out of the Christian community. It involves far more than programmed meetings and church attendance. Yet, structured learning is an important element necessary for healthy Christian growth. As such, those responsible for education within the church must utilize whatever means and resources that are available to develop meaningful programs. These learning endeavors should help people to fulfill their calling as Christians. Both the educational process and content should be relevant to learner's needs. These needs will vary with age and background of the participants. Those planning adult education activities need to utilize a developmental perspective in the coordination and implementation of programs.

Pastoral Care

An understanding of faith and adult development has several important implications related to pastoral care. First, church leaders should be alert to the needs of those going through transition periods. During such times people may feel less secure and in need of personal encouragement and support. In recent years, for example, much attention has been given to men and mid-life crisis. Men in their late thirties and early forties may require additional and specific support related to the developmental needs of that period. But it is important to recognize that adults of all ages go through transition periods where they experience increased stress. In addition, particular events such as becoming parents, changing jobs, and having children leave home, should cue the pastor to be on the lookout for emerging needs. People respond to events differently. What may seem normal and routine for one, may cause another personal trauma.

Second, what affects one family member has implications and repercussions for every other family member. Pastoral care should be geared to the family and not to just individual members. For example, it is possible to overlook the needs of children when dealing with a developmental need of a parent. Yet the child probably has been affected by that need in some way as well. Sunday School teachers can play a supportive role in providing care to the children.

Third, an understanding of adult development can help individuals better understand and prepare for their own development. Instruction in this area is one form of preventative counseling, which can also help family members to appreciate the different issues other family members may be facing as well as those faced by friends or other loved ones. It can also assist individuals in understanding that many of their own personal concerns are not unique to them, but are shared by others as well.

Fourth, such knowledge has implications for pastoral counseling. It helps the pastor to place particular issues and concerns in a developmental perspective. This can help to provide a framework both for understanding specific issues and for developing strategies related to problem solving.

Fifth, pastors should be alert to the special needs of the elderly. Some older adults, especially widows, suffer from feelings of loneliness. Yet these individuals often have both the desire and the time to contribute to the work of the church. Not only can such involvement be a healthy experience for those in later adulthood, but they can make a significant contribution to congregational life and ministry.

In summary, a developmental perspective of faith and adulthood provides important insights related to pastoral care and counseling. Special attention should be given to those going through transitions as well as to family members. An attempt should be made to involve older adults, not only in congregational activities, but in ministry projects.

Evangelism

This study found that most individuals who became Christians during adulthood, did so during the midst of a transition experience. Many of these people had attended church as a child, but dropped out after they left home. Some, though, had never attended church.

A number of events prompted individuals to look to God for help. Marital problems and health concerns played a major role in this respect. Several people became Christians following marital problems or a divorce. Some individuals began to look for a church after they became parents, since they began to feel the need to do something for their children. Several others became Christians as young adults after they left home for the first time. Feelings of loneliness, lack of direction or feeling socially rejected all played a role in seeking Christ. For most of the individuals described above, either a friend, spouse, or relative played a major role in their conversion experience.

These findings have important implications for evangelism. Often, if a church has any evangelistic strategy at all, it is oriented to ''whosoever will." Generally, it is not targeted to any particular group. However, based upon this study, it would appear that those individuals who are experiencing some change in their life structure are more open to the gospel than people who feel more stable and secure. Churches should consider developing outreach programs to minister to those going through life transitions. Special target groups might include the divorced, widows and widowers, new parents, or the unemployed. For example, a parent training class could be conducted monthly which could meet one night a week for four weeks. Special invitations and related support information could be mailed or personally delivered to new parents. Similar approaches could be developed for the other groups mentioned focusing upon their particular needs.

Individual members of the congregation should also be trained to share the gospel in relationship to developmental needs and issues. The church needs to abandon evangelistic gimmicks and canned questions as approaches to sharing the gospel. Such approaches violate the very essence of the good news. Rather, the church needs to focus upon responding to life needs. People respond to the gospel because they are seeking life. Everybody has a need at some level. Many people have needs related to career, family life, or health concerns. When individual Christians are able to relate the gospel to life needs in an authentic way, evangelism is going to occur. This must be done in both word and deed. A developmental understanding of faith and adulthood can aid that process.

Summary and Concluding Remarks

In summary, a developmental perspective of faith and adulthood has implications for many areas of congregational life including preaching, education, pastoral care, and evangelism. Not only can such an understanding help individual Christians grow and mature, but it can also be an effective tool in helping them to understand and relate to the needs of others.

It is my hope that the life stories and focus upon faith within this book will encourage you to grow closer to Jesus Christ. Those who encounter him are changed forever.

> Therefore, since we are surrounded by such a great cloud of witnesses, let us throw off everything that hinders and the sin that so easily entangles, and let us run with perseverance the race marked out for us. Let us fix our

eyes on Jesus, the author and perfecter of our faith, who for the joy set before him endured the cross, scorning its shame, and sat down at the right hand of the throne of God. Consider him who endured such opposition from sinful men, so that you will not grow weary and lose heart. (Heb. 12:1–2)

END NOTES

Chapter 2

[1]Erik H. Erickson, *Childhood and Society,* 2nd. ed. (New York: Norton, 1963).

[2]Else Frenkel–Brunswick, "Adjustments and Reorientation in the course of the Life Span," in *Middle Age and Aging,* ed. Bernice Neugarten (Chicago: University of Chicago Press, 1968), pp. 77–84.

[3]Daniel Levinson, *The Seasons of a Man's Life* (New York: Knopf, 1978).

[4]Ibid., p. 19.

[5]Ibid., p. 84.

[6]Ibid., p. 30.

[7]Ibid., p. 192.

Chapter 3

[1]Siegfried Giedion, *Mechanization Takes Command* (New York: Oxford University Press, 1948), p. 43.

[2]Levinson, p. 41.

[3]Alan B. Knox, *Adult Development and Learning* (San Francisco: Jossey-Bass Publishers, 1977), p. 59.

⁴Richard H. Williams and Martin B. Loeb, "The Adult's Social Life Space and Successful Aging," in *Middle Age and Aging,* ed. Bernice Neugarten (Chicago: University of Chicago Press, 1968), p. 380.

⁵Robert J. Havighurst, *Developmental Tasks and Education,* 3rd. ed. (New York: David McKay Company, Inc., 1972).

⁶Donald Guthrie, *New Testament Theology* (Downers Grove: Inter-Varsity Press, 1981), p. 574.

Chapter 4
¹James Fowler, *Stages of Faith* (San Francisco: Harper & Row, 1981), p. 32.

²See Rudolf Bultmann, *Theology of the New Testament,* vol. 1, (New York: Charles Scribner's Sons, 1951), pp. 314-329; idem, "The pistis Group in the New Testament," in *Theological Dictionary of the New Testament,* vol. VI, ed. Gerhard Friedrich (Grand Rapids: Wm. B. Eerdmans Publishing Company, 1968), pp. 203-228.

Chapter 5
¹James Fowler, *Stages of Faith* (San Francisco: Harper & Row, 1981).

²Peter Berger and Thomas Luckmann, *The Social Construction of Reality* (New York: Anchor Books, 1967), pp. 92-108.

³Leonhard Goppelt, *Theology of the New Testament,* Vol. 1 (Grand Rapids: William B. Eerdmans Publishing Company, 1981), pp. 141ff.

Chapter 9
¹Michael P. Farrell and Stanley D. Rosenberg, *Men at Midlife* (Boston: Auburn House Publishing Company, 1981).

Chapter 11
¹Charles S. Harris, *Fact Book on Aging: A Profile of America's Older Population* (Washington, D.C.: The National Council on the Aging, Inc., 1978), p. v.

²Ibid., p. vi.

³Robert N. Butler, "Successful Aging," in *Life Span Development,* ed. Martin Bloom (New York: Macmillian Publishing Company, Inc., 1980), p. 356f.

⁴Harris, p. 71.

⁵Ibid., p. 32.

⁶Jeffery Turner and Don Helms, *Life Span Development* (Philadelphia:

W.B. Saunders Company, 1979), p. 452.

[7]Linda George, *Role Transitions in Later Life* (Monterey: Brook/Cole Publishing Company, 1980), p. 58.

[8]Harris, pp. 98–99, 143.

[9]Helena Znaniecka Lopata, *Women as Widows* (New York: Elsevier, 1979), p. 261.

[10]Phyllis R. Silverman, "Widowhood and Preventive Intervention," in *Life Span Development,* ed. Martin Bloom (New York: Macmillian Publishing Company, Inc., 1980), p. 380.

[11]James A. Peterson and Michael P. Briley, *Widows and Widowhood* (New York: Association Press, 1977), p. 47.

[12]Lopata, p. 293.

Chapter 12

[1]Carles Corr, "Reconstructing the Changing Face of Death," in *Dying: Facing the Facts,* ed. Hannelore Wass (New York: Hemisphere Publishing Company, 1979), 1979), p. 11.

[2]Jeanne Q. Benoliel, "Dying in an Institution," in *Dying: Facing the Facts,* ed. Hannelore Wass (New York: Hemisphere Publishing Company, 1979), p. 140.

[3]Corr, p. 11.

[4]Ibid., p. 31.

[5]Victor M. Marshall, *Last Chapters* (Monterey: Brooks/Cole Publishing Company, 1980) p. 78.

[6]Corr, p. 52.

[7]Corr, p. 52; Marshall, p. 82.

[8]Marshall, p. 120.

Chapter 13

[1]Emil Brunner, *The Divine Imperative* (Philadelphia: Westminster Press, 1947), p. 385.

[2]Dietrich Bonhoeffer, *Ethics* (New York: The Macmillian Company, 1969), p. 254.

[3]Brunner, p. 388.

[4]Reuben Hill "Decision Making and the Family Life Cycle," in *Middle Age and Aging*, ed. Bernice Neugarten (Chicago: University of Chicago Press, 1968), pp. 286–295.

[5]Joan Aldous, *Family Careers* (New York: John Wiley & Sons, 1978), p. 81.

[6]Paul Hiebert, "The Flaw of the Excluded Middle," *Missiology: An International Review* 10 (January 1981): 47.

[7]James M. Fowler, *Stages of Faith* (San Francisco: Harper & Row, 1981), pp. 191f.

Chapter 14
[1]Cyril O. Houle, *The Inquiring Mind* (Madison, WI: University Press, 1963).